THE ERA
OF CHARLEMAGNE
Frankish State and Society

STEWART C. EASTON
AND

HELENE WIERUSZOWSKI
Professor Emeritus of History
The City College of New York

THE ANVIL SERIES
under the general editorship of
LOUIS L. SNYDER

ROBERT E. KRIEGER PUBLISHING COMPANY
HUNTINGTON, NEW YORK

To our former Colleagues
in the History Department
of the City College of New York

Original Edition 1961
Reprint Edition 1979

Printed and Published by
ROBERT E. KRIEGER PUBLISHING COMPANY, INC.
645 NEW YORK AVENUE
HUNTINGTON, NEW YORK 11743

Printed in the United States of America

Library of Congress Cataloging in Publication Data

Easton, Stewart Copinger, 1907-
    The Era of Charlemagne.

    Reprint of the edition published by Van Nostrand, Princeton, N.J., which was issued as no. 54 of An Anvil original.
    1. France—History—To 987.   2. Charlemagne, 742-814.   I. Wieruszowski, Helene, joint author.   II. Title.
[DC73.E2   1979]   944'.01   79-4518
ISBN 0-88275-905-1

National Series Data Program
ISSN #0570-1062

PREFACE

It has been the purpose of the authors of this book to provide an analysis of state and society in Western Europe in the time of the Frankish rulers of the Carolingian house, concentrating their primary attention on the reign of Charlemagne, or Charles the Great.

Both the French and the Germans claim Charlemagne as their national hero and the founder of their national institutions. But Charles, of course, built on the work of his predecessors. It has, therefore, been found essential to give some consideration, however brief, to the preceding centuries, going as far back as the fifth century, when the Franks, under Clovis, the first Merovingian monarch, were consolidating their power in Roman Gaul with the conquest of the last Roman territory in that province.

By extending their study back into the fifth century the authors were compelled to come to grips with some of the most thorny and controversial problems of European historiography. This period is often superficially referred to as a "transition" between ancient and medieval times; but this concept begs a number of important questions. How much, for example, of Roman civilization survived the destruction that followed in the wake of the Germanic invasions? What were the chief factors leading to the numerous changes in political, social and economic life that occurred in Frankish society after the long period of anarchy and confusion? What were the main symptoms of this later development in earlier times? How far back in Roman history can they be traced? Was the Frankish society really a new one? Or was it the result of the integration of some of the components of the Roman and Germanic heritage?

If the authors were to attempt to reach conclusions on all these questions, after giving full consideration to all that modern scholarship has contributed to their solu-

3

tion, obviously more space would be needed than is available in this book. All that they can, therefore, hope to do is to integrate and sum up the results of the scholarly work of such eminent historians as F. Lot, M. Rostovtzeff, H. Pirenne, A. Dopsch, A. Pfister, L. Halphen, R. Lopez, R. Baynes, to mention only some of the most important names; and to use their own best judgment in deciding how to fill in the picture and in choosing the emphasis to be placed on the Carolingian achievements. In selecting the documents for the second half of the book, they have tried to find new material in addition to the material customarily included in source books of medieval and modern history.

But when all possible consideration has been given to the notion of the continuity and integration of ancient civilization, and to the concept that this civilization provided the building blocks for the social and political structure that we call medieval, it must be admitted that after all Frankish civilization as it emerged in the time of Charlemagne was a new one—if only because its geographical boundaries and its racial components were different. As we pursue the history of this era we see the centers of political life and civilization shifting from the Mediterranean to western and northern Europe, northern and central Italy, western Germany, and to England, southern Scotland and Ireland. When Christianity was taken to regions outside the Roman Empire, the peoples of these lands were trained to accept the ways of Roman civilization, including the intellectual heritage of the Greeks and Romans, even though they had been totally unaffected by the way of life of these ancient peoples. Whatever they accepted they transformed in accordance with their own customs and traditions. From whatever angle one looks at the Carolingian age, without doubt it was the "First Europe" that was born in this period. Bearing this in mind the authors have written this Anvil book in the hope that it might contribute to the general knowledge of a most significant chapter of European history.

H. W.
S. C. E.

TABLE OF CONTENTS

5

Part I—THE ERA OF CHARLEMAGNE:
Frankish State and Society

— 1 —

THE MEROVINGIAN KINGDOM

Consolidation of the Frankish Realm under Clovis. The Roman records speak of the Franks for the first time about the middle of the third century. The name is applied to a number of Germanic groups settled in the lower valley of the Rhine. Some subdivisions of the Franks were called Salians, meaning, in the Romance vernacular, "peoples of the coast." About a century later, the Roman emperor Julian allowed the Salians to settle as *foederati* (allies), from Toxandria (North Brabant) to the Schelde river. The region between the Rhine delta and the Schelde remained their homeland. Soon their territories were spread out so that they were bounded by a line from Dunkirk to Maestricht. In due time this line became the linguistic boundary between the Flemish- and the Walloon-speaking Belgians.

Another large group of Frankish tribes was known as the Ripuarians, a name likewise suggesting inhabitants of the sea coast. These tribes crossed the Rhine early in the fifth century and gave aid to the Roman general Aetius, who was engaged in fighting the Huns. Thereafter, they founded an independent kingdom on the left bank of the Rhine, with Cologne as their capital. By this time (455-460) the Salians were again on the move, sprawling out to the Somme river at the expense of the Roman Empire. But shortly afterward one of their tribal kings, Childeric, son of Meroveus, later to become the legendary hero who gave his name to the Merovingians, found it convenient

9

for reasons of policy to attach the fortunes of the Salians to those of the declining Romans. He helped a Roman *magister militum* Aegidius and his son Syagrius to maintain a precarious rule in the neighborhood of Soissons and to defend the line of the Loire against the aggressive Visigoths in Aquitaine. The "kingdom of Soissons," as it was called, was in fact the last region in Gaul to be retained at least nominally under Roman authority. Childeric, its Frankish supporter, lived in Tournai, where his tomb was discovered in 1653.

Soon after his father's death in 482, Childeric's son Clovis, while still very young and sharing military rule over the Salians with nine other chieftains, took advantage of the death of the Visigothic king Eurich, his most formidable potential enemy, to attack the kingdom of Soissons, which he conquered in 486. He followed up this victory over Syagrius by further invasions of Roman territory until he reached the Loire River and the borders of Visigothic Aquitaine. In this process he captured three major urban centers—Paris, Orleans, and Reims—and a fourth, Soissons, to which he transferred his residence from Tournai. Thus, the former kinglet of Tournai had now outdistanced his rivals, the Goths and Alemanni, in the race for northern Gaul, and laid a firm basis for a Frankish kingdom in Roman Gaul.

But Clovis still had to reckon with the rivalry of his fellow Salian chieftains, to say nothing of the resistance of his own warriors and followers. These did not permit their leaders to exercise unrestricted rule, but claimed the right to share in political decisions as well as in war booty. Step by step, through murder, intrigue, and fratricidal wars, Clovis disposed of his Frankish relatives until, as he himself complained, he was left without any kin in the world. He subjected the recalcitrant Frankish freemen to the same methods of government that he had learned to exercise over the conquered Gallo-Romans, who had been accustomed to a strictly centralized rule under the Romans. The possession of the Roman fiscal land which had fallen into his hands, of the abandoned estates whose owners had fled or been killed, and of the remaining cities, with their tax-paying middle class, made the new king of the Franks irresistible. From a Germanic leader, whose relation to his followers was a personal one and involved mutual obligations, he had been transformed before their eyes into the absolute despot of a large territorial state, and heir to the Roman machinery of government.

As Clovis's conquests carried him deep into Gallo-Roman areas, with the lines of Frankish settlers thinning out as he moved farther from his Salian homeland, with only small war bands and his bodyguard to protect him, he was compelled to treat the native population with caution and consideration. At first he treated the Romans under his rule fairly, later allowing them a status equal to that of the Franks. They were admitted to the highest offices in State and Church, as well as in the army. Integration between the German conquerors and the conquered Romans proceeded smoothly and almost without friction and prolonged the life expectancy of the Regnum Francorum—thus presenting a marked contrast to the contemporary Italian kingdom of Theodoric the Ostrogoth, whose work was ruined by an internal conflict within the dual state that he tried to uphold.

The most important single step in the stabilization of the kingdom of Clovis was undoubtedly the conversion of the monarch to the Catholic faith of his Roman subjects in preference to the Arian creed * of the other Germanic kings ruling in Gaul. The conversion and baptism of Clovis occurred at about the same time as—probably shortly before—his conquest of the Alemanni (496-497). By this conquest he eliminated these aggressive rivals from the control of the upper Rhine plain and subjected most of them to his rule. No doubt the conversion was more for political than doctrinal reasons, since it enabled him thereafter to pose as the champion of orthodoxy against the Arian "heretics" and won him the support of the influential Roman clergy and of the Roman senatorial nobility from which most of the high clergy was chosen. Thus fortified, Clovis turned against the Arian Visigoths and put an end to the rule of the Visigothic kings of Spain in Aquitaine. This province, which was the most flourishing and culturally advanced part of Gaul, the later Merovingians regarded as their most precious possession. It was so

* Arian creed: the doctrine that Christ was not the eternal son of God nor of the same substance.

valuable that in the division of the kingdom after the
death of Clovis, each of his four sons secured a share of it,
rather than allowing it to fall as a whole into the hands
of any one of them.

Clovis himself did not live to see the whole of Gaul
united under his rule. The conquest of the kingdom of
Burgundy (southeastern Gaul) was the result of the combined efforts of his sons (534). Provence was claimed by
Theodoric for his Italian kingdom and was won briefly
by him as a result of aid given to the Visigoths in their
wars with the Franks. But Witigis, the successor of Theodoric, granted it to the Franks in return for aid given to
him by the sons of Clovis in his own wars with Byzantium.
Merovingian Gaul with the acquisition of Provence gained
a much desired outlet to the Mediterranean. Clovis had
succeeded in uniting the Frankish tribes on the left and
right banks of the Rhine, the remaining Salians whose
lands he claimed by right of kinship, the Ripuarians, and
the Chatti (Hessian Franks). All these Frankish tribes,
together with the Alemanni, who occupied territories to
the left and right of the Rhine (Alsace and Suabia),
formed a solid bridge to the peoples of inner Germany,
thus providing the foundation for the task of spreading
Christianity and ancient learning to these areas.

It is sometimes said that Clovis moved to the Île de
France from his Salian homeland for the purpose of
breaking with the folk tradition of his people, and he is
credited with the intention of imitating the superior traditions of the Roman people in preference to those of his
Germanic ancestors. But this is a misunderstanding of his
policy. Far from abandoning his German heritage he must
be credited with having those parts of the Salian tribal
laws written down which scholars consider the most ancient part of the famous *Lex Salica.* He granted to all his
subject peoples the right for all future time to be tried by
their own law. He believed he had been chosen as the
special instrument of God to lead the Church to victory
over her enemies, as he expressed it in the Prologue to the
Lex Salica, and he took steps toward organizing the Frankish church under his leadership. The first Frankish synod
was convoked by him at Orléans in 511. He was willing to
accept from the Byzantine emperor the title of consul, and

the gift of a cloak and diadem, bestowed upon him by the ambassadors of Emperor Anastasius during his war with the Visigoths and Ostrogoths.

Though Clovis displayed these insignia in a public ceremony, it was certainly not as a token of submission to the emperor, as some scholars have concluded. His purpose was solely to demonstrate to the Gallo-Romans that the emperor approved of his conquests. Nothing was further from Clovis's mind than any thought of the recognition of "Rome" as his overlord, whether in the person of the emperor or of the pope. On the contrary, the first Merovingian with care and perspicacity laid the foundations both of an all-Gallo-Frankish realm and of a Frankish national church. These were to be inherited by the Carolingians.

The Successors of Clovis. After the death of Clovis his sons divided the kingdom in accordance with German custom. The center of the whole kingdom and of each subdivision remained the Ile de France ("kingdom" of Syagrius). This was the square comprising the four capitals—Paris, Soissons, Orléans, and Metz, one to each son —together with the rich fiscal land of each. Aquitaine, as already noted, was partitioned, each son receiving a part as an annex to his share in the north.

The emphasis of the foreign policy of the sons of Clovis was the attempt to strengthen and extend the Frankish kingdom as a whole. Theudebert I, the ablest of the Merovingians after Clovis, tried to secure northern Italy for his house. He was the first Frankish king to strike his own gold coins as a sign of sovereignty. He also assumed the name of Augustus. In a bid for an imperial world position he even prepared to attack Byzantium by land, but the enterprise, when it was taken over by his weaker son, could not be carried to a successful conclusion. Nevertheless, Theudebert himself showed considerable diplomatic skill in taking advantage of the struggle between the Byzantines and Ostrogoths in Italy to increase Frankish power. This is the first example of the imperial universalism that later characterized the Italian policy of the German kings.

Of more practical importance was the establishment of direct or indirect Frankish rule in large territories of inner Germany. The western part of the kingdom of the Thuringians was conquered. The Thuringians were allowed to keep their own tribal law (*Lex Thuringorum*), but were ruled by Frankish dukes, who among other tasks had to collect a tribute in the form of hogs from the Thuringians. This tribute was still paid to the German successors of the Merovingians as late as 1002. Riots often made it difficult for the Franks to maintain their rule, since the Thuringians were strengthened by the Saxons, who had settled north and northwest of Frankish Thuringia in a kind of semidependence. The Franks were able also to extend their rule over the Bavarians, who were a loose group of heterogeneous peoples, then moving into what was to be their permanent homeland between the Danube River and the eastern Alps. At the same time they strengthened their rule over all the Alemanni.

The appointment of Frankish dukes in Bavaria had the result of loosening rather than cementing the relations between the Bavarians and their Frankish rulers. The dukes were inclined to identify their interests with those of the subject peoples. Although elections were still held as a formality, they in fact ruled by hereditary right. In particular the Agilolfingians, descendants of a Frankish official who was a native of Burgundy, were instrumental in the formation of a kind of self-made tribe, which tended, as did the homogeneous Alemanni, to break away from their Frankish overlords. At the turn of the sixth and seventh centuries, when the Irish missionary Columban visited Alsace, part of the homeland of the Alemanni, a region between the Vosges mountains and the Rhine, and when he visited the vicinity of the Lake of Constance, he found the Alemanni or Suabians roaming the forests, living in their old barbarous fashion, untouched by Christianity and faithful to their old heathen customs and rites. It was not until the age of the Carolingians that the Church was able to make substantial advances in these areas, and confirm the conquest with missionary and civilizing activities.

The Saxon problem remained unsolved throughout the Merovingian period. The raids of the Saxons and their kindred Frisians into the Frankish Rhineland regions created a military problem for the weakening Merovingian state that was too much for its resources and abilities. Unable to check the raids and migrations, the Merovingians had to content themselves with the imposition of an annual tribute of four hundred cows on some of the Saxon tribes in Thuringia. Yet, in spite of the danger of permitting these warlike and riotous neighbors to remain on their right flank across the Rhine, their presence in fact may well have enabled the tottering Merovingian state and society of the seventh century to survive. For unlike the Ostrogoths, who found themselves after their occupation of Italy uprooted and completely separated from their German co-nationals on the other side of the Alps, the Franks on the left bank of the Rhine constantly drew reinforcements from the tribes across the Rhine. This infiltration by Germanic groups helped the Franks to resist Romanization and ensured the preservation of their German folkways, language, and literary heritage—a strong contrast to the conditions in northern France, which the Merovingians had made their permanent center.

Historians estimate that the Germanic element in the region between the Seine and the Loire in the sixth century did not amount to more than from 15 to 20 per cent of the whole population. For a long time the region remained bilingual. The co-existence of Germanic and Roman elements for such an extended period of time has left a profound impression on the French language, which contains a large number of Frankish words drawn not only from the political and military vocabulary of the Germans but also from the ordinary words in everyday use. But the Frankish adaptation to Roman customs in some areas speeded the process of Romanization, which appears to have been completed in the Ile de France by the early eighth century. This led to the establishment of the linguistic boundary line as it exists today, running roughly from a point of the Flemish coast between Somme and Schelde to the Meuse, and along this river to the Jura Mountains and the Alps. North and east of this line, in the old Frankish homelands where the German population formed a majority, the few remnants of former Roman settlements were quickly absorbed. Linguists have shown that the word *deutsch* appears first in the late seventh century somewhere along the linguistic boundary, and desig-

nates the "popular" language of the Franks in contrast to
the vulgar language (Latin or Romance) spoken in the
Romanized regions. It is from the region called Austrasia,
north and east of this line, that the Carolingian family
hailed. They drew most of their revenues from this area,
and here they wielded great political power as leaders of
the Austrasian aristocracy.

Background of Carolingian Ascendancy. After the
death of the last son of Clovis, Clothar I, who reunited
the kingdom after the death of his three brothers, it was
torn to pieces by fratricidal strife, and the family was
almost wiped out. For a period the warring parties were
headed by two queens, Fredegunde and Brunehilde, who
raged against each other and their respective kin with
relentless cruelty. Brunehilde as a demon of hatred was
the model for the character of her namesake in the
Nibelungenlied, while the struggle between the rival
queens found its way into the main plot.

The aristocracy was able to take full advantage of the
opportunity provided for it by this internecine warfare.
The Merovingian strength was almost exhausted by the
time of the death of Queen Brunehilde. It was the Austrasian and Burgundian aristocracy that restored the
Neustrian Clothar II to the throne. Thus, the unity of the
kingdom was restored, but under the direction and control of the aristocracy. Leaders of the Austrasian nobles
were a certain Bishop Arnulf of Metz and Pepin the
Elder, mayor of the palace in Austrasia. It is significant
that these two ancestors of the Carolingians contributed
to the limitation of the Merovingian power not only by
giving their consent to the rule of the king but by placing
him under constitutional restraints.

In 614 the council of bishops and magnates dictated
terms to Clothar which were the price he had to pay for
his dignity. These concessions are included in a Precept
of Clothar, and in the Edict issued at Paris in 614, which
many have considered to be a "Magna Carta" of the
Frankish nobles. Although the comparison with the Charter of 1215 is certainly an exaggeration, it is true that a
kind of compact or law had been imposed on the Merovingian kings. But solemn pacts and edicts were hardly
necessary as a means of controlling the later Merovingian

kings. Physical exhaustion and moral and intellectual de-
generation had already incapacitated the royal family,
who had little option but to turn over all real authority to
the mayors of the three separate parts of the old Regnum
Francorum, Austrasia, Neustria, and Burgundy. These
mayors continued the struggle for power either in the
name of their respective Merovingian puppets or in their
own name—and either with or against the aristocracy of
the kingdoms they represented.

Toward the end of the seventh century Pepin of Heristal, a scion of the house of Bishop Arnulf and Pepin the
Elder, emerged as mayor of the palace in Austrasia. He
defeated his opposite number of Neustria in the battle of
Tertry (687), imprisoned the king of Neustria, and had
himself installed as mayor of the palace by the nobility of
all three kingdoms. This gave the dynasty later to be
known as the Carolingians the virtually undisputed ruler-
ship over the Frankish lands in Gaul and Germany.

Frankish Institutions in the Merovingian Era. The
most important institution of the Franks was the monarchy. The king, following in the footsteps of the Roman
emperor, was the government in his own person. He issued laws and decrees, appointed the officials, decided on
war or peace, dispensed justice at the highest level, and
levied taxes and tolls, making use of the Roman system of
taxation as well as of the bureaucracy that collected them.
The king had, therefore, entirely eliminated the assembly
of freemen which, under tribal custom, had shared in political activities. He was as much of a despot as was possible in that era. No man dared challenge his actions; any
opposition offered to him by Franks who resented their
loss of freedom was ruthlessly suppressed. (*See Readings
Nos. 1*A *and 1*B.) He treated his own German warriors
and followers in exactly the same manner as he treated the
conquered Romans. Germanic customs such as the royal
ban originally used for control of the army were later
used for the maintenance of peace in the public interest.
The payment of *fredus* (peace money) for the violation
of the ban increased his strength at the same time as it
added to his resources.

The court, which was identical with the central government (*palatium regis*), consisted of the royal guard (*an-

trustiones), household officials, and followers who had commended themselves to him. All these men were the king's *leudes* and enjoyed a special protection (*munt, mundium*) which carried with it triple *wergeld,* or composition money.* In the course of time the king's household officials tended to become also public officers of state. The administrator of the royal estates (*domesticus*), for example, in time took over duties similar to those of a chief minister of state when he became mayor of the palace. The king's private secretary (*referendarius*) at the same time headed the chancery that despatched letters and charters and worded the capitularies, or royal decrees.

The Franks took over the Roman district system of the *civitates* in Gaul and imitated it beyond the Rhine. Some 150 among the urban centers of these districts had survived the onslaught of the barbarians. The *civitates* were now known as *pagi* (Germ. *Gaue*) and were ruled each by a count (*comes*) who represented the king in all political and judiciary functions. (*Comes* was originally the title of a Roman military official.) Since the king and not the assembly was now the supreme judge, the count replaced the former elected official (*thunginus*) in both the regular and irregular courts (*mall, malberg, placitum*). Above the count, however, was the king's own court, presided over by the king, and later by the mayor of the palace. The local bishop often acted as assistant judge (*auditor*). The count's income consisted of a portion of the feud and peace money (*faidus* and *fredus*) paid within his area of jurisdiction, together with a percentage of the revenue from the royal estates.

The principle that all freemen were equal in their obligations as well as their rights gave way soon after the conquest to a legal system of social gradation. On the *villae* or estates there were now three scaled groups the lowest of which were the slaves (Latin *servi*). A slave could be enfranchised by various procedures and join the class of freedmen (*liberti,* Germ. *liti*); above the *liberti* were the peasants, *coloni,* who were free only in theory, since they were tied to their holdings in the *villa.*

* *Wergeld:* in early Germanic law, the price to be paid by the kindred of a manslayer to the kindred of the slain person as composition to avoid the blood feud.

Above these three groups came the freemen, Franks and other Germans, who "professed" their own hereditary law. At the time of the conquest there had been no nobles among Clovis's Franks. The most important development of the sixth century is the rise of a new aristocracy of both German and Roman origin. It is true that at first the Roman landholders were not given equal status with the Frankish freemen. Though not dispossessed of his land and income, a Roman paid half the *wergeld* of a Salian Frank. But ownership of land as well as service in all offices to which they were freely admitted gave these Romans equal status with the newly arising Frankish service aristocracy, the king's *leudes:* they became part of the group referred to in the laws as *homines Franci.* On the other hand, "immunity," the privilege attached of old to the senatorial *latifundia* became soon applicable not only to the royal fisc and the land of the Church but also to that of the royal *leudes.* By the turn of the sixth and seventh centuries this new nobility (*proceres, potentes, priores*) not only controlled local politics but claimed the right to participate in the affairs of the kingdom and of the royal dynasty. The Roman and German elements had by this time become almost completely integrated; the Romans felt like Franks and adopted German names, while the Germans had adopted Roman ways of life and the Romance language. In 614, they were able to dictate to King Clothar II the conditions under which he was to be permitted by them to rule the now reunited Regnum Francorum. (*See Readings Nos. 1*C *and 1*D.)

The clergy, as landowners and political leaders in their cities and immunities, closely coöperated with the secular magnates. They fully shared the latter's desire for independence through limitation of the king's power. Recruited as they often were from the old Roman senatorial nobility and from the new Germano-Roman service aristocracy, they were naturally bound to the secular magnates by *esprit de corps.* Nevertheless, they had also complaints of their own. They objected to royal interference with canonical procedure in episcopal elections, they resented royal limitation of the power of ecclesiastical courts, and above all they objected to simony. The king did not yield on all points, but he did guarantee both property and independence to bishops and counts, that is, to the two officials whose work provided a measure of coherence and order in the rapidly disintegrating Frankish society of the seventh century. He assured the bishops of canonical elections (*a clero et populo*), but he would not prohibit simony, nor did he promise to refrain from appointing members of the court to bishoprics, He conceded to the local magnates the right to have judges (counts) chosen from among the land-owners of the districts they were to administer.

Hitherto, the counts had been the king's representatives. Now they became hereditary lords of their districts, and as such they dispensed justice in their own right, for the king could no longer check or depose them. In his Paris Edict, Clothar II also allowed his power of taxation to be restricted—a prerogative, incidentally, that tribal kings had never possessed, but which had been usurped by Clovis for himself and his successors, after the model of the Roman government. From the beginning the free Franks had vigorously protested against being required to pay the *tributum,* a poll tax paid by all classes of unfree men in the Roman Empire, holding that their status as freemen was seriously impaired by such an imposition. In the Edict of 614 the poll tax is not mentioned; but the king had to promise not to introduce any new land taxes (*census*). The same restriction was placed on the king's right to levy tolls, market dues, and other commercial ex-actions, which had indeed been arbitrarily increased, since they were among the most important sources of income for the royal treasury. Though the document as a whole did not impose excessive demands on the king, it re-mains true that a Frankish monarch condemned abuses of his own power, thus creating a precedent for the su-premacy of law over a ruler which "has never been for-gotten since" (A. Pfister).

Economic Changes in the Merovingian Age. The resistance of the landowners to paying taxes tells only a part of the story of the decrease of royal revenues in this period of semianarchy of the seventh century. The Mero-vingians lacked the trained bureaucracy necessary to ad-minister the complex system of Roman taxation. Royal grants to churches and magnates diminished the revenue from tolls and other commercial exactions, and the mint-ing of coins, an important source of revenue for the Roman emperors, shows a picture of complete confusion. Moreover, revenues such as tolls and market dues depended on trade, above all trade with the East. The trade of the southern cities of Gaul with the East seems already to have greatly diminished in late Roman times, and never recovered fully. There were brief periods of recovery, it is true. Gregory of Tours frequently refers to foreign merchants, Syrians, Greeks, and Jews, in old Gallic trade centers such as Marseilles and Orléans. They traded products of local industries for Byzantine silk, papyrus, and Oriental spices. But the extent of this trade and its influence on the economy of Frankish Gaul has been greatly exaggerated by Henri Pirenne, who based his theory of the continuity of Mediterranean culture on the rather sparse evidence for this trade, combined with evidence for the continued circulation and use of money.

The continuous growth of an agricultural economy and the concomitant decline of the urban centers is a phenomenon that scholars have noted as typical of the later centuries of the Roman Empire as early as the age of the Antonines. The settlement of the barbarians on Roman soil must surely have accentuated rather than weakened this tendency. As one symptom of the decline of urban life in the seventh century it may be noted that the cities of northern Gaul ceased to serve as the residences of the Frankish counts and as centers of administration. It is after all not surprising that the Franks were not able to restore an institution that the Romans themselves in part had allowed to go out of existence.

The primary motive for the conquest of Gaul by the Franks had been land hunger. Immense tracts of land had fallen into the hands of the king by right of conquest, and it was therefore in the form of land that the king made awards to his followers, and paid such "salaries" for services as were needed. At first the revenues from land more than covered the costs of maintenance of the royal family and court. Money was something foreign to the experience of the invading barbarians. They had no idea how to put money to use for the encouraging and furthering of trade, and they gave scant attention to the ports and roads which they had inherited. Internal factors such as these and

others provide a sufficient explanation for the changes in
the life of Western Europe during the seventh century,
even before the Saracens made their conquests in the
Mediterranean. In later centuries the Saracens may have
speeded up these developments; but it is certain that they
did not set them in motion. It will be noted also later in
this book that trade was not completely absent from the
economic life of the Carolingian age. So the Saracens were
not, as Pirenne contended, responsible for the cessation
of trade in the centuries that followed their conquests.

The Church in the Merovingian Age. The most important institution of the Frankish kingdom was the
Church. In an age of anarchy it provided the only moral
force and leadership. The people saw the bishops and
priests as dispensers of the sacraments and the miraculous
and supernatural forces that they identified with the Divine. Clerics also contributed civic services of great importance to the cities which had become the diocesan sees.
At a time when the magistrates and councils went out of
existence in one city after another, the clergy alone provided some public services and upheld some degree of
public order. In an age when crimes remained unpunished
though committed quite openly, the clergy felt doubly responsible for the souls committed to their care. Yet even
the clergy could not escape the effects of the general moral
decay and the complete absence of any provision for the
enforcement of public law. (*See Readings Nos. 2*A *and
2*B.)

The secular powers gave the clergy little assistance. The
kings and mayors of the palace looked on the Church as
a source of revenue and an instrument of power rather
than as an institution for the spiritual welfare of their
subjects. From the early seventh century it became normal
for them in spite of the assurances given in Clothar's Edict
to sell high Church offices to the highest bidder, mostly
laymen, who entirely lacked religious qualifications and
education. At the same time the rulers, who were by this
time running short of the land necessary to pay their followers, attempted to strip the Church of its revenues.
Land was even "confiscated" from the Church to train and
equip a cavalry force to meet the Saracen armies in southern France. Against such inroads the clergy found itself

helpless. Rome had never been allowed to interfere with the Frankish Church, which had always been controlled by the state. An appeal to Rome would therefore have been useless—as useless as an appeal to the impotent monarch of the Franks himself. The kings, indeed, had ceased to play a significant part in the life of the Church. Clovis, as has been noted, called a Church synod at Orléans in 511. But when in 742 the Anglo-Saxon missionary Boniface called another such synod, no similar council had been held in the kingdom in more than eighty years.

Learning and Education. It need hardly be mentioned that during the Merovingian period, learning and education were at their lowest ebb. Even in the formerly renowned centers of Aquitaine, which in the sixth century had produced outstanding writers like Avitus of Vienne, the poet Venantius Fortunatus, and especially the historian Gregory of Tours, the light of learning was extinguished toward the end of the Merovingian age. It is necessary only to glance at Merovingian manuscripts to recognize to what degree the Roman script had been corrupted before the Carolingian reform, and the knowledge of Latin deteriorated. (*See Readings Nos. 3A and 3B.*) The thorough reform of cultural life of which Merovingian society was so greatly in need had to wait for the work of the Anglo-Saxons and Carolingians in the eighth century. The way, however, was prepared when about the year 590 a group of Irish missionaries under St. Columban began the work of restoring monastic discipline and rigid asceticism. These Irish missions worked among the pagans in rural areas in some parts of Frankish Gaul. But their influence was not limited to the great monasteries they founded, nor to their work among the pagans. They spread the spirit of asceticism even among large groups of the aristocracy. The monasteries of Luxeuil and Fontaines in Burgundy, founded by the Irish monk Columban, and that of St. Gall on the Lake of Constance, founded by Columban's disciple Gallus, continued the tradition of learning and literary instruction that had been the heritage of Irish monasticism ever since Irish monks had planted their famous monasteries in Scotland and the north of England in the later sixth and early seventh centuries.

THE GROWTH OF THE CAROLINGIAN EMPIRE

Consolidation of the Frankish Realm: The Defeat of Islam. Although Charles the Great has bestowed his name on an important epoch of European history, and the adjective Carolingian (derived from his name) has been attached to a "renaissance" as well as to an empire, his life and work would have been unthinkable without the solid foundations laid by his father, grandfather, and great-grandfather. Charlemagne was fortunate enough to have an uncle who preferred the sanctity of a cloister to the cares of a ruler in a violent age, and his own brother died prematurely. Like his father King Pepin, Charles was enabled to inherit after a brief interval an undivided realm instead of the divided estate to which all but a few Germanic rulers were condemned in the early Middle Ages. Charles was much more fortunate than his grandfather Charles Martel (the Hammer), who was an illegitimate son and not intended by his own father, Pepin of Heristal, to inherit the mayoralty which he himself had held so long and so successfully.

Robbed by a natural death of one son and by an assassination of the other, Pepin of Heristal had hoped that his six-year-old grandson, his only legitimate heir, would inherit his position, and his widow Plectrude would be able to govern "discreetly" until he came of age. But Plectrude was unable to keep her husband's natural son Charles, who was already a grown man, in the prison to which she had consigned him. He escaped, gathered some troops around him, and after an initial defeat was able to restore the Frankish united kingdom as it had existed under Pepin. Having reduced the aristocracy to obedience, and put a Merovingian scion of neither ability nor importance on the throne, according to the custom of his house, he was ready to defend his realm against the many dangers

24

that threatened it—not only the usual Saxon incursions from the north and attacks from the dissident duchies of Alemannia and Bavaria, but a new menace from the south, the expanding Saracens who had entered Spain in 711, three years before the death of Pepin of Heristal.

Fortunately for the Frankish position in the south, Eustace, the duke of Aquitaine, was able to keep his duchy from falling into the hands of the Saracens, although the invaders were able to capture a number of important strongholds in the southeast of France (Septimania). At first Eustace was not inclined to accept the authority of Charles Martel in his duchy, but found he could not maintain his position without his help. Faced by a formidable Saracen leader, Abd-ur-Rahman, he appealed to Charles, who with a strong army met the Saracens in the vicinity of Poitiers in 732 and defeated them, killing Abd-ur-Rahman and putting an end to the immediate danger to his own domains.

This Frankish victory, also known under the name of the battle of Tours, permitted the eighteenth-century historian, Edward Gibbon, to indulge in an eloquent disquisition on the possible effects of a Muslim victory, which included the imposition of Islam on all western Christendom and the substitution of Islamic theologians for Christian in the halls of Oxford. But nowadays it is recognized that the Muslim invasion of northern Aquitaine was but an extended raid and that even without meeting such a Christian champion as Charles Martel, the Saracens did not possess the manpower necessary to consolidate any eventual victory in France. It is, therefore, extremely doubtful whether the battle of "Tours" should be regarded, as it once was, as one of the great decisive battles of the world —important though it undoubtedly was for the prestige of Charles, who was widely regarded as the savior of Christendom.

Indeed, two years later, the Saracens penetrated into Languedoc, and for several years thereafter they remained within the Frankish borders in Septimania. But whenever Charles was able to bring major forces to bear on them, he was able to drive back the Saracen raiders and their reinforcements, and force them back into Spain. In 738 Liutprand, the Lombard king, undertook the task while

Charles was away in Saxony. He was equally successful. Later in the century Charlemagne was able to conquer part of Spain itself and establish the Spanish March.

Charles Martel made good use of the Saracen menace in bringing southern France under his effective control. When Duke Eustace died in 735, his son took an oath of fidelity to Charles; and though the actual fidelity was somewhat indifferent, there could be no doubt thereafter as to who was the master in southern France. Charles appointed counts and representatives in the territory who were responsible to himself. He likewise established his full authority over the Frankish Church, and did not hesitate to lay hands upon ecclesiastical domains and revenues when he had need of them for the defense of the country. When his puppet Merovingian died in 737 he did not trouble to nominate a successor, but ruled as a king, without the title. The pope addressed him as sub-king (*subregulus*), an accurate enough title; but he never aspired to the title of king—perhaps because he was an illegitimate son of Pepin of Heristal, or perhaps because he was too busy to trouble about such niceties as the title by which he was known. He possessed as much power as he could conveniently use already. So he remained mayor of the palace, leaving it to his son to claim and receive the more noble title.

End of the Merovingian Kingdom. Before he died in 741, Charles Martel divided his domains between his two sons, Carloman, the elder, and Pepin, the younger, called the Short. Among other territories Carloman inherited Austrasia, while Pepin received Neustria. At once the aristocracy rose in revolt against the central power. Aquitania and Bavaria, independent duchies which had not been bequeathed by Charles to his sons, and the province of Alemannia threw off the yoke that had been imposed on them by Charles, while the Saxons began a campaign of pillage on the frontiers. The lords were not disposed to accept the authority of a mere mayor of the palace. To a true Merovingian monarch they might owe some duty, or at least respect, even though in recent years they had in fact ceased to obey them. It was a distinct advantage to the lords to have a monarch on the throne who was unable to enforce his will, even while his very presence prevented anyone else from holding the title. Carloman and Pepin, fully appreciating the situation, filled the vacancy on the throne by elevating Childeric III, an obscure Merovingian, who duly recognized them as his mayors. (*See Reading No. 4A.*) But the practical effect of the legitimization of their authority was negligible. For six years they campaigned until the various revolts were suppressed and the lords were restored to their obedience. Then in 747 Carloman abdicated in favor of his brother, who from that moment appears to have recognized that the time had come for him to inherit the legitimacy of rule that had hitherto rested in the feeble hands of the Merovingian puppets. Carloman's preference for the monastic life was not shared by his son, who had been deprived of his inheritance by his father's abdication. For a time this young man disputed his uncle's right to sole rule, but he proved unable to overthrow Pepin, who had by this time consolidated his position.

It was, of course, possible for Pepin to send the last Merovingian to a monastery on his own authority and to have himself crowned a king. But such a procedure would in no way have enhanced his authority. What he needed, like Napoleon in a later century, was to have his actual power recognized as legitimate. The Merovingians were unquestionably legitimate, and only a power superior to all earthly rulers could be considered entitled to replace the Merovingian line. Such a power was the Church, whose authority as representative of God and successor of St. Peter had recently been greatly enhanced by the extensive missionary work of St. Boniface and his associates. If the pope were to agree to consecrate Pepin as king, then his rank would be higher in the eyes of Christian mankind than that of any duke or count, however noble their lineage. He might reasonably hope to pass the rank down to his descendants, perhaps saving them from having to undergo such trials as his own campaigns of six years' duration. According to the records, in 750 Pepin sent a delicate inquiry to Pope Zacharias through a bishop and an abbot. The emissaries were to ask the pope if it was right that a prince without power should bear the title of king. (*See Reading No. 4B.*)

To understand the import of this request, one has to

look at the situation of the papacy at that particular moment. The popes had been experiencing much difficulty with the Lombard kings, who had been encroaching on lands claimed by the pontiff. Already in the time of Charles Martel, the pope had addressed several "tearful" pleas to the mayor of the palace to aid him when Liutprand, the Lombard monarch, was at the gates of Rome. But Charles, grateful for the aid given him against the Saracens by his Lombard ally, had responded negatively. Now a new Lombard king, Aistulf, was making a serious attempt to unify Italy under his rule and had already captured Ravenna, capital of the Byzantine exarchate, in northeastern Italy (751). It was certain that in due time the papacy would be in need of an ally. The pope could not count on his official overlord in Constantinople, whom, in any case, he disapproved of as an iconoclast. There was only one source of possible support against the Lombards—the Franks, who had always been Catholic Christians from the time of the first Merovingian king and had sufficient force at their disposal to defeat the Lombards. The message from Pepin must, therefore, have appeared to Pope Zacharias like a gift from heaven. After a decent interval he responded in kind that, in his opinion, it was better for him who held the real power also to hold the royal title.

Thereupon, Pepin summoned an assembly of Frankish notables who duly elected him king. This act of election, a Frankish custom, was then followed by a religious ceremony, in which a papal emissary (St. Boniface?) anointed the new king with oil after the manner of the ancient Hebrew kings, a practice that had already been adopted in the Visigothic and Anglo-Saxon kingdoms. The last Merovingian monarch was then despatched to a monastery, there to end his unimportant days (752).

Relations with the Papacy: "The Donation of Pepin." The following year Pope Zacharias died, to be succeeded by Stephen II. Almost at once Aistulf began to threaten the Holy City, and Stephen determined to obtain the aid of the new king of the Franks. Still not wishing to insult the emperor, his titular overlord, too openly, he sent an embassy at the same time to the iconoclast in Constantinople, expecting little and receiving in reply instructions to threaten the Lombard king with the emperor's wrath, but nothing otherwise of substance. The message to Pepin met with full success. Pepin invited the pope to pay a personal visit to him at Ponthion in France. After completing the hazardous journey Stephen entered into negotiations with Pepin that resulted in an alliance with the Frankish monarchy. Pepin promised under oath to give the pope assistance, and to support the "claims" of the see of St. Peter in the "Roman Republic" and other Byzantine territories of central Italy. (*See Reading No. 5A.*) The pope addressed the king as *patricius Romanorum,* a title hitherto held by the Byzantine duke of Rome, whom the Frankish king was now to replace as protector of the see of Rome and of "the Romans." Stephen then repeated the ceremony of anointing Pepin and anointed his sons also.

These preliminaries over, Pepin took steps to implement the new alliance. He called an assembly of his magnates at Kiersy near Laon, and the campaign against the Lombards was agreed to by the assembly. It was at Kiersy also that Pepin issued a "document of donation" in which the promise of Ponthion was made more explicit though probably not yet entirely defined in terms of territories, boundaries, and rights. Essentially it gave "to St. Peter" the duchy of Ravenna (called the Exarchate) the province south of it known as the Pentapolis ("the five cities"), and the duchy of Rome, all territories that were still legally Byzantine, and, at least in theory, ruled by the Byzantine exarch in Ravenna, on behalf of his master in Constantinople.*

It took two expeditions by Pepin to compel Aistulf to relinquish the disputed territories. After the first expedition had resulted in a victory for Pepin and the submission of Aistulf, the Lombard monarch merely waited for Pepin to return across the Alps. Then he marched on Rome itself, forcing the pontiff to send a pitiful appeal to his protector on behalf of himself and St. Peter. The pope also complained that Aistulf had broken the promise he had given after Pepin's first expedition, in that he had "not allowed to return to the Blessed Peter so much as a

---

* For the details of the various donations see the much fuller account in the introduction to Reading 5.

single handful of earth." (*See Reading No. 5B.*) In 756
Pepin returned and taught the Lombard king a severe
lesson. This time he was compelled to yield the Byzantine
territories he had conquered. Pepin thereupon drafted a
document embodying his official donation "to the Holy
Roman Church and all the future pontiffs of the Apostolic
See." This, at least, is what the papal biographer asserts—
though the actual text has never been brought to light,
and if it ever existed it has long ago disappeared. The
king then sent his representative, Abbot Fulrad of St.
Denis, to receive tokens of submission and the keys of
the ceded cities. (*See Reading No. 5C.*) The abbot then
deposited the documents on the tomb of St. Peter.

Naturally, the Byzantine emperor complained bitterly
of these donations, but he was unable to obtain any satis-
faction. Pepin replied to the Byzantine emissaries that he
had been fighting not for the "sake of man, but for the
love of St. Peter and the remission of his sins," and he
had no intention of taking the lands away from the Holy
See, on which he had just bestowed them.

The Donation of Pepin laid the foundation for papal
rule over a wide strip of land from the Tyrrhenian Sea
across the Apennines to the Adriatic. But Stephen and his
successor Paul I did not obtain effective possession of
more than a small part of the territory at this time. A new
Lombard king, Desiderius, refused to give more than he
was compelled to, and Pepin at the time was in no position to do more than exercise diplomatic pressure on the
Lombard and make what arrangements he could. It was
not until Charlemagne confirmed the Donation of Pepin
in a solemn document (774) (*see Reading No. 5D*), after
he had extinguished the Lombard kingdom, that all the
territories promised to the pontiff at last passed under his
control, together with others that had not formed part of
the Donation of Pepin. Seven years later Pope Hadrian I
was complaining to Charlemagne that he could not obtain
secure possession of the Sabina, in the southeast corner
of the duchy of Rome, because of "the machinations of
wicked men." (*See Reading No. 5E.*)

It was probably in the pontificate of Paul I that the
papacy revealed the existence of a document, later shown
to be forged, which purported to show that the first Chris-

tian emperor, Constantine I, after being healed of leprosy by Pope Sylvester I, had granted to the pope "all the provinces of our city of Rome, of Italy, and the regions of the West." (*See Reading No. 5F.*) Though the papacy was unable in the time of Charlemagne to make effective use of this document, in later centuries, when it had been somewhat hallowed by time, it was able to put it to profitable use.

Elsewhere Pepin was, on the whole, successful in his efforts to consolidate his kingdom. The duke of Bavaria for a time acknowledged Pepin's authority and aided him in his campaigns in Aquitaine, but later deserted the Frankish army and threw off his allegiance to the king. In Aquitaine Pepin had to fight a long war, but after the assassination of the duke, the duchy made its full submission to the Frankish monarchy. Pepin was able to take advantage of dissensions among the Saracens and finally drove them out of France, adding Septimania to his kingdom. Thus, when he died in 768, he left a relatively stable inheritance to his two sons, in spite of some unfinished business in Bavaria which had to be settled by Charlemagne. In dividing the kingdom between his sons Charles and Carloman he was, of course, only following German custom; but in doing so he disregarded the old divisions of the Merovingian kingdom, in the hope that his sons would be willing to coöperate in the defense of his now much larger territories.

Charlemagne: Character and Personality. The division of Pepin was actually one that might well have caused friction between the brothers, since Carloman, the younger brother, received the larger portion of the old Merovingian lands, including the most settled territories of the kingdom. Charlemagne had only the outer provinces along the Atlantic coast from the south of Gaul to the estuary of the Rhine, including the frontier territory of Thuringia. Aquitaine was divided between the brothers.

Almost immediately a revolt broke out in Aquitaine, which Charles had to suppress by himself, since Carloman refused to help him. Carloman also disapproved of Charles's marriage to the daughter of Desiderius the Lombard king, since Lombardy bordered on his own territory in the east. The brothers likewise disagreed on papal as

well as on Lombard policy. When Charles found it impossible to work in harmony with Desiderius, who was
again interfering in papal affairs, he repudiated his Lombard wife and married an Alemannian princess, thus giving his brother an opportunity to cause further trouble for
him. But at this moment (771) Carloman providentially
died. Desiderius offered asylum to his widow and children
in the hopes of causing difficulties to Charles. The latter,
however, took firm steps to place under his control the
entire domain of his late brother, and thereafter ruled
alone the whole kingdom of Pepin. The stage was set for
the expansion of the Frankish realm and ultimately its
conversion into the Carolingian empire.

At the death of his brother, Charles was twenty-nine
years of age. According to Eginhard or Einhard, his biographer, he was tall—his height was seven times the length
of his foot, perhaps just under six feet—fair-haired, inclined to corpulence, fond of the chase and all outdoor
activities, a fine swimmer and a hearty eater, fond of
roasts, and unhappy when instructed by his physician to
eat only boiled meat. Unfortunately, Einhard's talents as
a biographer, which were remarkable for his time, are to
some degree marred by his desire to imitate Suetonius,
the Roman biographer of the Caesars. He has followed his
model closely, sometimes slavishly; and though the imita-
tion is an excellent one it might have been more useful
for posterity if he had chosen his material somewhat more
judiciously and occasionally exercised his critical judgment. The biography is too external a picture to enable
us to gain any profound understanding of his subject, and
the modern writer must therefore try to give depth to the
portrait by a more thorough consideration of his character as revealed by his actions.

Charlemagne, of course, was a semibarbarian ruler,
coming from a region (Austrasia) which had been only
lately Christianized and little influenced by Roman civilization. In inner Germany he ruled over completely barbarian peoples. He was able, according to Einhard, to
converse in Latin and he understood Greek; but his native
language was German. He could not read or write. When
he tried to learn he was too far advanced in years to
achieve his goal. He was, however, eloquent and clear in

his speech, and there were enough literate men around him for him not to suffer from his own illiteracy. He appears to have been competent in the mathematics and astronomy of his day.

He was in all respects an absolute autocrat. The decisions made in his realm were all his, and he expected to be kept informed on all matters that concerned him. Einhard describes him as affectionate toward his immediate family and friends, though he treated his daughters as if they were his personal property, especially his three favorites. He insisted on having them always with him and refused to permit them to marry—in spite of rumors about their "chastity" current at the court, and the birth of an illegitimate son to his second daughter Bertha.

The absolutism of Charles, however, was always tempered by his conviction that he was responsible to God for the kingdom he had inherited. Not that he felt himself in any way responsible to the representatives of God upon earth. On the contrary, he regarded the Church and its clergy as subordinate to himself. He could not be indifferent to the morals and behavior of the clergy; he chose its representatives within his realm with as much care as he could. He expected them to perform their tasks with diligence and uprightness. In return he showered land and privileges upon the clergy. But he and his chancery deluged the members of the clergy from the highest to the lowest with both moral and secular advice; and there is little sign that any of them took it amiss or felt that he was in any way exceeding his authority as an earthly ruler. He aided the pope in his earthly ambitions when it suited his purpose and his interests. But he also did not hesitate to curb the pope's ambitions if he did not approve of them. He did his best to aid the Church in stamping out the incipient heresy of adoptionism.

His court name was David and there can be no doubt that he looked upon himself as a second David—though his private life may be thought to have been at least as close to that of Solomon. He was as steeped in knowledge of the ancient Hebrew monarchy as of the political thought of St. Augustine, whose *City of God* he caused to be read to him as often as time and his other duties would permit. Without doubt this fact is the key to his character and policy. He regarded himself as chosen by God to rule his kingdom and empire, that he was responsible to God for all that he had been granted, that he was a Christian ruler as David had been a Christian ruler before the coming of Christ. The realm which he had inherited was to be a Christian realm, and it was a part of his task to see that it was made ever more Christian. His Christian zeal was usually tempered by political common sense. He had no objection to dealing with Muslims when it suited his purpose. He did not approve either of the iconoclasm of the Byzantine emperors or of the excessive respect for icons favored by the papacy and by the empress Irene of Constantinople. He used his influence to modify the papal position in the controversy. He could be ruthless in his treatment of enemies. His behavior toward the Saxons whom he subjugated and converted by force must forever remain a blot on his record, even though in later years he somewhat relaxed his severity toward them. When policy dictated mercy and a more humane treatment of his enemies he was usually willing to be merciful, as long as the enemies submitted fully and completely to his will.

His military abilities, though considerable for his day, were in no sense remarkable. He always commanded forces superior to those available to his enemies. It was his ability to concentrate his forces and strike quickly that distinguished him rather than any strategic or tactical ability. The defeat suffered by his troops at Roncesvalles when his rear guard was destroyed by the Basques (Gascons) may be attributed as much to his lack of foresight as to any defect on the part of his commanders.

By modern standards Charles was, above all, an extremely simple man. There is no evidence of any imagination in him, and no startling innovations in any field can be attributed to him. If he dreamed of restoring a Roman Empire when all the institutions of the times were against the survival of such an archaic concept in the reality of the ninth and tenth centuries, this can be attributed to the fact that he and his advisers knew no other model. There was nothing illogical or unnatural in merely adding to the realm which he had inherited. The fact that before his death he announced his intention of dividing it among his sons demonstrates that he had neither wish nor expectation that it would be preserved intact as a single empire ruled by one prince after his death. In this he deviated in no respect from Germanic custom. It was natural in later times, when the lands that he ruled fell into anarchy and Europe was split into many fragments, that his reign should be looked back to as a golden age of Western European unity, enhancing the luster of his posthumous reputation. But it may be doubted whether it was his own personal abilities and achievements that influenced posterity to grant to him alone the privilege of having the word "great" incorporated in his name (Carolus Magnus—Charlemagne). It is true that he towered above the Western world in his day; but it may also be stressed that his contemporary, the caliph Harun al-Rashid of Bagdad, did not consider an embassy from Charlemagne, which figures so prominently in Frankish annals, worth mentioning in his own records.

Expansion to the North and East. Perhaps the most enduring work of Charles was the expansion of his realm to the east and northeast. For many years the Saxons had raided into the Frankish lands. No ruler before Charlemagne had done more than repel the raids and mount occasional punitive expeditions. The Saxons were still pagans and held stubbornly to their old traditional Germanic deities. They had no desire for conversion; on the contrary, they were violently anti-Christian. Their pride as a people rested upon their belief in the superiority of their own gods. They knew that conversion to Christianity would mean subordination to the Frankish monarchy, if not to a totally alien papacy. For the same reason in a later century the Bulgars hesitated long and tried many avenues of escape before they agreed to accept Orthodox Christianity and to come under the spiritual and temporal authority of Constantinople.

For twenty-three years of his reign Charlemagne warred against the Saxons. Time after time he would defeat the Saxon armies and compel their leaders to accept his authority and give hostages. They would even accept under duress the activity of Frankish missionaries in their midst. Then, when Charles had retired, they would triumphantly throw off the yoke, massacre as many of the Franks as they could, including the missionaries, and return to their own beloved religion. When Charles's outposts in Saxony were insufficiently garrisoned, the Saxons would fall upon them and were thus able to inflict many damaging defeats upon the Frankish king. So Charles came gradually to recognize that there would be no peace until the whole of Saxony was subjugated and converted to Christianity.

Charlemagne's methods of conquest became both more systematic and more cruel, and he imposed a kind of martial law on all Saxony. He built and equipped forts to keep the peace in the conquered areas and to serve as outposts for further expansion. He compelled the conversion of the Saxons, imposing the death penalty on all those who refused. He extended the same death penalty to the Saxons who refused obedience to the behests of the Church, and to those who continued to keep many of their old pagan customs which were especially abhorrent to Charles. Heavy fines were exacted for lesser infringements of his edicts, which ordered that all pagan practices were to be brought to an end. After a rebellion by the Saxons, Charles had 4500 Saxons executed. The Church was permitted to exact its tenth (tithe) from all the conquered peoples. (*See Reading No. 6A.*)

This policy of ruthlessness did not escape criticism from Charles's most intimate and trusted advisers. Alcuin, in particular, drew attention in a letter to the truth that "faith is an act of will and cannot be enforced." Alcuin even went so far as to suggest to Charles himself that the unaccustomed tithe should not be exacted at the same time that the Christian religion was forced upon the people. (*See Reading No. 6B.*) Though Charles somewhat softened his rigor in later years, either because it was proving unsuccessful or because of the criticism it received from such men as Alcuin, he continued even as late as 802 to engage in devastations and mass deportations. Only when three new bishoprics were established under the jurisdiction of the archbishop of Cologne for the purpose of spreading the faith by more peaceful means did the Saxons become gradually reconciled to their lot.

As a by-product of the Saxon wars Charles finally subdued the Frisians who occupied the greater part of the territory now called the kingdom of the Netherlands. The Frisians, like the Saxons, were devoted to their old gods,

but Christianity had been planted in Frisia, though somewhat insecurely, by the predecessors of Charles. When
Charles was fighting the Saxons, a number of Frisians,
devoted to the old gods as well as to their own freedom
and independence, joined the Saxons, thereby providing
the Frankish ruler with the opportunity and the excuse to
conquer them completely and force conversion upon the
whole country.

Bavaria, unlike Frisia and Saxony, was already Christian. Charlemagne did not, therefore, have to convert the
Bavarians as he "converted" the Saxons. But he had many
disputes with the Bavarians over matters of religious organization. Tassilon, the Bavarian duke, merely wished to
retain his personal independence and that of his duchy,
together with control over the Bavarian clergy. He had
no desire to be dominated by the Frankish monarchy.
Though permitted to retain his independence for a period,
the time came when Charles felt himself strong enough
to compel the formal submission of the duke, and in particular to bring his religious policies into conformity with
those of the king. Tassilon temporized, pretending to submit, but in reality working against Charles and the Franks,
with the consequence that he lost the support of his own
people, who regarded him as a breaker of oaths. Charles
was, therefore, able to have him condemned as an oath
breaker without having to wage formal war against him.
Tassilon was legally deposed by his own lords, and Charles
annexed his territory. Thereafter Bavaria, whose forms of
independence were respected by Charles, became a loyal
part of his dominions and could be used as a safe spring-
board for the subsequent expansion to the east and the
campaigns against the Avars.

Beyond the German territories stretched the lands of
the Slavs and the Avars. Charles made no effort to convert
the Slavs to Christianity, although he engaged in several
military expeditions against them. All the Slavic peoples
in the vicinity of the Elbe submitted to the authority of
Charles and became his vassals. Thereafter they were left
in peace as long as they fulfilled their not very onerous
obligations. The Elbe itself Charles kept as his frontier,
fortifying strong places on the left bank of the river. In
due time the frontier was left to the care of his counts

of the march (margraves), to be defended by them on behalf of the monarch.

The Avars were treated with less consideration than the Slavs. These people occupying a region roughly corresponding to the later kingdom of Hungary, were a permanent threat and danger to all their neighbors. Charles had no wish to make them Christians, but he did not propose to tolerate their unwanted presence so close to his dominions—and especially not when they supported the rebellious duke of Bavaria against him, as they did in 787. In a series of campaigns, some carried out from Italy and in the hands of the sons of Charlemagne, the great treasure of the Avars, kept in a fortified circle or ring, was captured. The treasure was put to good use by Charles, and helped to increase the prosperity of his kingdom, making possible much of the cultural progress of his later years, as well as helping to finance his further campaigns. The clergy was very doubtful of the possibility of converting such a truly barbarian people as the Avars to Christianity, but met with unexpected success when it was decided to use gentle persuasion rather than the force utilized against the Saxons. The Avar khan, contrary to expectations, became a loyal ally of Charles and was finally himself converted in 805, thus completing the subjugation of the erstwhile scourge of central Europe, and the incorporation of their western territory into the Frankish Empire. One of the two marches which Charles organized in this region, the Pannonian march in the north, was to become the core of medieval Austria (Ostmark).

Wars in Spain: The Spanish March. Charles was early determined to complete the work of his father and grandfather and push the Saracens farther into Spain. The disturbed internal conditions of Muslim Spain presented easy opportunities for Frankish intervention. Charles, in fact, invaded Spain at the request of one of the Muslim factions; but since it did not prove to be the stronger one, he was held up in front of Saragossa on the Ebro and was unable to take the city. Finding himself deserted by his Muslim allies, and hearing of a Saxon uprising which urgently demanded his presence, he retreated over the Pyrenees with the main body of his troops, leaving his rear guard to follow. This rear guard was set upon

by the Basques or Gascons, a fiercely independent people
who lived on both sides of the Pyrenees and owed a nominal allegiance in Spain to the Saracens. These warriors
cut the Frankish rear guard to pieces in the defile of
Roncesvalles in 778, earning a posthumous fame for the
defending Count Roland of the Breton march, who died
in the battle. (*See Reading No. 7.*) He was subsequently
celebrated in the *Song of Roland*.

This was probably the most serious defeat ever suffered
by the Franks in the reign of Charlemagne, so severe,
indeed, that Frankish chroniclers hesitated to give it its
due importance while Charlemagne lived. The monarch
returned as soon as he could and began a systematic
conquest of northeastern Spain. Ultimately, in the last
years of his reign, his sons were able to establish the
Spanish March, which was to become later the kingdom
of Navarre, northern Aragon, and the county of Barce-
lona. The purpose of the March was to serve as a fortified
area for the defense of the Pyrenees and southern France.
The Basques in France and Spain gave their formal allegiance to the Emperor, in exchange for the maintenance
of most of their privileges and liberties.

Intervention in Italy. At the time of Pepin's death
the Lombards had suffered serious losses, but were still
far from ready to submit completely to the Franks. They
continued to present a threat to Rome, whenever the
Franks were not at hand to defend it. In the early years
of the reign of Charlemagne the situation deteriorated rapidly, since Desiderius, the Lombard king, was able to
take advantage of the rivalry between Charles and his
brother Carloman and to keep Carloman's two children
as hostages after the death of their father. So when a new
and vigorous pope, Hadrian I, appealed to Charles to
intervene to protect the cities given to him by Pepin, which
were slowly being wrested from his control by Desiderius,
Charles crossed the Alps and defeated the Lombard king,
shutting him up in Pavia. As soon as Charles knew that
the city would fall, he made his way to Rome for extended
discussions on the future of central Italy. There he was
treated with great honor and greeted by the title of patrician, which he had held for twenty years but never used.
When the Lombard king finally surrendered Charles him-

self became king, thus adding the title "King of the Lombards" to that of "King of the Franks." He later had his infant son crowned king of Italy by the pope (781).

The negotiations with Hadrian were protracted, and the pope was far from winning all he had hoped for. Charles would not allow him to extend his territories at the expense of his own new kingdom of the Lombards. But he did agree to allow the pope to round out his Roman territories, giving the former duchy of Rome the boundaries which it retained until 1870. (*See Reading No. 5E.*) For the rest, Charles became a more effective king of the Lombards than any of the earlier Lombard kings, and whatever authority the popes exercised in central Italy during his lifetime outside the duchy of Rome was exercised by royal permission. Papal interests were subordinated to those of the monarch.

There can be little doubt that Charles looked upon the pope, in spite of his spiritual overlordship of Christendom, as a useful assistant in temporal matters, as long as the pope fell in with his wishes, but that at times he also looked upon him as a dangerous rival to his own rule in Italy. It was thus a part of his policy to give the pope certain relatively minor territories to keep him occupied and to provide him with adequate revenues, while making certain at the same time that he was never in a position to challenge his own rule. There is no reason to suppose that Charles ever listened to the papal pleas on any grounds other than his own political and military interests. This was as true of the strong pope Hadrian I, whose letters are full of complaints against Charles, as of Pope Leo III, Hadrian's successor, who owed everything to Charles and was never in a position to challenge his royal protector, even though it was he who placed the imperial crown on the head of Charles on Christmas Day, 800.

Coronation of Charles as Emperor. When Leo III was elected pope in 795, Charles had occupied the Frankish throne for twenty-seven years. No sooner had Leo been elevated to the papal throne than Charles sent a messenger to Rome with instructions and letters. Both contained admonitions on how the monarch expected him to act, how he expected him to pray for him, intercede with God for the success of his arms, and generally to keep his own house in good order. He told the pope that he ought to govern the Church of God in the spirit of piety, and reminded him that the honor he held was but a transitory one in comparison with the heavenly reward that awaited those who labored well for the Church. (*See Readings No. 8*A *and 8*B.)

The new pope, however, was in an insecure position in Rome. Lombard opposition was, of course, now a thing of the past. But, as was so often to happen in the future, a second party of Roman clerics, aided by nobles, wished to see its own nominee on the papal throne. From the beginning of Leo's reign there were disturbances and disorders in Rome, always an unruly city, culminating in an attack on the person of the pope in 799 by a band of conspirators. They accused Leo of adultery and perjury and attempted to tear out his tongue and eyes.* Only with difficulty was he rescued by representatives of the Frankish monarch. From his refuge he addressed a piteous letter to Charlemagne, which reached the monarch while he was deep in Saxony.

At once Charles invited the pope to visit him for the purpose of giving him a personal explanation of what had happened. Leo met the king at Paderborn in Saxony, whither his accusers followed him soon afterward. Alcuin, the king's leading adviser, was probably influential in persuading Charles to take no action against the pope on the charges made by his opponents. At all events, Charles sent him back to Rome under the care of two archbishops. The latter heard the charges and acquitted the pope, and the conspirators were sent to France for punishment. The spectacle of a humiliated pope unquestionably augmented the already exalted notion of the position of their master held by Charles's courtiers, and they now recognized, as Alcuin put it, that upon Charles alone "rested the welfare of the Church." (*See Reading No. 8*C.)

The following year Charles himself went to Rome and made a ceremonial entrance into the Holy City about the end of November, 800. He then presided over a special assembly of notables, lay and clerical, in which the pope

* Einhard asserts they actually did this (*see Reading No. 8*H), but it is evident from Leo's subsequent career that they were unsuccessful in their attempts.

was permitted to clear himself by an oath of the charges against him. Two days later there followed what may be considered as one of the most significant and important events in Western history—the coronation of Charlemagne as emperor in St. Peter's. There is no dispute about the facts. While Charles was praying, before the celebration of the Mass, Pope Leo approached him. As he was rising, Leo placed a crown on his head, while the Roman people cried three times, "life and victory to Charles Augustus, crowned by God, great and pacific emperor of the Romans." Then the pope kneeled before him and "adored" him, according to the ancient protocol of the late Roman emperors. (*See Readings No. 8*D *to 8*H.)

Where the difference of opinion among scholars has arisen is in determining whose was the initiative in this event—whether it was all arranged by Charles himself and his entourage, or whether it was the pope who took the step without prior consultation with and the prior knowledge of Charles. Opinions range from those of the French scholar, Louis Halphen, who has argued that Charles had planned the step for some time and that the ceremony had been carefully arranged in advance with Pope Leo, to Karl Heldmann, who insists that "never would the Frankish king have aspired to the rank of the Roman emperor . . . had not a specific event served as the direct cause for such an eventuality." The specific event, in Heldmann's view, was the opposition of the local Roman population to the person of Leo III as pope, and the desire of the latter to fortify his position. According to this view, Charles was elevated so that he could, like a Roman emperor, wield the supreme judicial authority in the empire, which empire would of course include Rome. Thus he would be in a position to punish Leo's detractors and to lend him the necessary legal power to maintain his position thereafter.

On the one hand there is Einhard's categorical statement that Charles was affronted and angered by the papal act (*see Reading No. 8*H), and that he would not have gone into St. Peter's on that day if he had had any inkling of the pope's purpose. On the other hand Charles's advisers, especially Alcuin, had in the years prior to 800 lost no opportunity to exalt the rank of their royal master. Words such as "Christian Empire" slipped from Alcuin's pen; he had already been called Augustus by a poet. Until fairly recently scholars used to concentrate on the importance of the Empire for the later history of the West. But modern scholarship, especially with the growth of Byzantine studies, has focussed attention on the manner in which the coronation of Charles usurped the rights of the emperor in Constantinople, who had never relinquished his position as overlord of Rome and the papacy. He and he alone was the successor of the great Roman emperors who had ruled both East and West. He could acknowledge no other ruler in the West as his equal. A king was wholly different in rank from an emperor. There could be many kings but only one emperor. Charles, in becoming emperor, was, from the Byzantine point of view, usurping a rank which could never be his; nor could a pope, himself subordinate to the emperor in Constantinople, presume to crown any king, however exalted and powerful. Thus, Leo, in crowning Charlemagne, had served final notice that he no longer acknowledged the emperor in Constantinople as the Emperor. It is difficult to believe, these scholars insist, that Leo would not have concerted such a move with his nominee, especially since he was totally in the power of the Frankish king.

Nevertheless, it is possible to reconcile the statement of Einhard that Charles disapproved of the coronation and the strong evidence that Charles had always intended some day to allow himself to be crowned emperor. Moreover, Charles himself made much of his new dignity after 800, even going so far as to exact a new oath of fidelity from "every man in his realm, down to twelve-year-olds." (*See Reading No. 12.*) What seems likely is that Charles disapproved of the manner in which the initiative had been snatched from him by a pope who only a few days before had been accused of many crimes and whose innocence was open to question in spite of the fact that he had cleared himself by an oath. Moreover, Charles was not yet ready to embroil himself with the emperor in Constantinople, where conditions at a later date might well be much more propitious for the delicate negotiations that would be necessary if a war were to be avoided. Charles knew that his new rank would have to be recognized by the emperor, and that he would have to pay some price for the recognition. It was, therefore, essential that he should be allowed to choose the most favorable moment. As it happened, the emperor Constantine VI was soon afterward deposed by his mother Irene, with whom Charles entered into marriage negotiations. But by that time everyone knew that it was his objective to obtain the recognition of himself as emperor and perhaps even unite the two empires. This the Byzantines would not permit. Irene herself was deposed, probably as a result of these negotiations, to be replaced by an emperor, with whom Charles was eventually compelled to deal. Recognition by the emperor cost him the city of Venice, recently captured by Charles's son Pepin. All this might have been avoided if Charles could have chosen his own time for his elevation and if he had not been compelled to accept the crown before his plans were completed.

History was to provide another reason why Charles might have resented the presumption of Pope Leo, although it is doubtful whether any of his contemporaries foresaw such an outcome, preoccupied as they were with the immediate events. The crowning of an emperor might well suggest to posterity that an emperor who was not crowned by a pope would be no true emperor. Thus, all later popes could look for protection from later emperors as their price for crowning them; terms could be exacted for the ceremony.

Even more portentous was the claim made by popes in later centuries that what a pope had given a pope could take away. Pope Gregory VII was to cite the coronation of Charlemagne as evidence of the papal right to appoint and depose emperors. It was a papal act that, indeed, had created the restored empire, thus demonstrating the superiority of the spiritual power to all earthly power, however exalted. If even the great Charlemagne had required to be crowned by the pope, so the argument ran, how much more any lesser monarch in the divided Europe of the eleventh century!

That Charles himself and his advisers may indeed have been aware of this implication is suggested by the fact that in 813, when he felt his end approaching and only one son survived him who could inherit his realm, Charles

had this son Louis crowned without the presence or sanction of the pope. Louis, however, went after all to Rome
to be crowned a second time, suggesting that he, at least,
felt that a certain sanctity was added to his title by a
papal coronation. Such was the success of the symbolic
act of Pope Leo III on Christmas Day, 800!

**Relations with Constantinople, Venice and the
Orient.** The rise of the Carolingian empire was naturally
disturbing to the rulers in Constantinople. The kingdom
north of the Alps presented no threat to the Byzantines.
It was far otherwise when Charles acquired the former
kingdom of the Lombards and aided the pope to consolidate his rule over the former Byzantine duchy of
Rome, for the Byzantines retained both important trading
interests and at least nominal rule over some of northeastern Italy, and over Italy south of Rome. Besides, the
emperor in Constantinople could not accept with equa-
nimity the notion that there was now a second emperor
in Europe; and a succession of Byzantine emperors had
no mind to recognize the title, not at least without exacting a considerable price for their recognition.

The empress Irene, who was on the Byzantine throne
at the time of the coronation of Charles, may herself have
seriously entertained the notion of uniting the two empires
by marrying Charlemagne. But her court would have none
of it, and, as we have seen, she was probably deposed because of her marriage negotiations which deeply offended
the court. When she was succeeded by Nicephorus, the
latter at first continued but soon rejected negotiations with
Charles over a pact that would have implied recognition
of Charles's imperial title.

Pepin, king of Italy, one of Charles's sons, therefore
undertook to wage war against the Byzantines. On the
whole the war went favorably for the Franks, but Pepin's
resources were strained by trying to fight on two fronts—
northeastern Italy, where he was generally successful, and
southern Italy, where the most that could be achieved was
a short-lived alliance with the prince of Beneventum, who
for a time aided Pepin in the war. The prince acknowledged Charles's suzerainty and separated himself from
Byzantium; but before the end of the ninth century when
Basil I of Constantinople reconquered most of southern

Italy, his princedom again entered into an alliance with Constantinople, with whom it carried on most of its trade. All the southern Italian cities regarded the Franks as powerful barbarians, who might be used and, if necessary, appeased for a time. But none would have been anxious to exchange the often nominal and seldom oppressive rule of the Byzantines, with whom they were in constant relations, for rule by a totally alien group of German barbarians. Thus southern Italy never became part of the Frankish domains, nor was it ever subjected to German imperial rule save for a few years in the end of the twelfth century and the first half of the thirteenth.

In the northeast the Franks were able to conquer Istria and some Dalmatian coastal cities and compelled the capitulation of Venice. This was a very serious matter, both for Venice herself, which was to a large degree dependent on Byzantine trade, and for the Byzantine emperor, who was unable to fight back effectively since he was fully occupied nearer home with wars against the Bulgars. On the other hand Charles ought to have recognized, as he apparently did not, the importance of possessing such an excellent seaport as Venice in the east of his dominions, giving his empire free access to the Adriatic. He seems to have been not only weary of the war—his son Pepin died in 810—but extremely anxious to obtain recognition of his title of emperor before he died. He may well have been somewhat senile by this time and willing to pay whatever price was asked of him for the sake of peace and recognition.

At all events, when the Byzantine emperor showed that he was willing to negotiate, Charles met him more than halfway, and the negotiations were concluded quickly. Charles restored Venice, the recent conquests on the Dalmatian coast, Liburnia, and Istria, which had been in Frankish hands for many years, and the new Byzantine emperor Michael accorded him the recognition of his title as emperor. (*See Reading No. 9.*) Venice, thus liberated from the Franks, was able, with the friendly support of the Byzantines, to make short work of her competitors in this area and completely shut off the Frankish empire from the Adriatic. Indeed, the astonishing career of Venice may be said to have dated from the treaty of Charlemagne with the Byzantine empire.

There is need only for a brief mention of the relations between Charlemagne and the caliphate in Bagdad. Since the Abbasid caliph of Bagdad was struggling to destroy his rival, the Ommayad caliph of Cordova in Spain, with whom Charles was also at odds, the Abbasid caliph, Harun al-Raschid, was a natural ally for Charles, since their interests were identical. Ambassadors were therefore exchanged between Aachen and Bagdad. The caliph sent Charles a number of expensive presents, including an elephant and a clock. Harun conceded to Charles certain rights of protection over the Holy Places and over pilgrims to the Holy Land—rights of which he was hardly able to take advantage, but which may have been valuable in that the caliph at the same time consented to improve the lot of Christians in his domain. Such relations with the caliph of Bagdad, whose power had reached its zenith in his reign and whose culture was far superior to anything known in the West, certainly increased the prestige of Charles. Unfortunately the elephant, which was greatly cherished by the king, died prematurely, after having lived out its few years as his inseparable companion.

In the dark age that fell upon Europe in the ninth century it was a long time indeed before such amenities as the exchange of presents between the Western emperor and the Oriental monarch appeared again in Western annals. The reign of Charlemagne was to prove but a brief interlude in European history. The Roman Empire could not be restored, nor was the time yet ripe for a new enduring Christian empire under Frankish leadership. Out of the ruins of the Carolingian empire was to emerge at last the key political institution of the West, the national state, a denial and negation of the Roman idea of unity.

But even the germ of the first national state was yet many years in the future; and the imperial idea was to die very hard, a lingering death that was not consummated until 1806. It was the fragmented nation-state that was the actual legacy of the Carolingian era to Europe, even though the reign of Charles himself appealed to generations of popes and emperors—to say nothing of poets and political scientists—as a golden age when Western Europe was one and undivided. The historian Nithard was already to write as early as the mid ninth century that Charlemagne at his death had "left all Europe in the greatest happiness."

It need hardly be added that hard-pressed Europeans in the twentieth century, looking back upon the thousand years of fratricidal wars that have filled the centuries since Charlemagne, still wistfully envy the Carolingian achievement of peace and unity, and look forward hopefully to its resurrection through abandonment of that sovereignty which in the ninth century was exercised by him alone, but which after his death came to be exercised by states called "national" which competed with one another for their share of the inheritance.

— 3 —

STATE AND SOCIETY OF THE FRANKS AT THE HEIGHT OF THE EMPIRE

Dopsch and Pirenne Theses. The traditional view of historians, long unquestioned, held that after the "fall of Rome" in 476 there was a pronounced break between all that had existed during the Roman Empire and what followed afterward. In particular, it was too often assumed that with the progressive barbarization and destruction of Roman institutions in the West trade dwindled to a mere trickle.

Modern historians, with access to far more facts than their predecessors, have laid this assumption peacefully to rest. But there remains the question of the extent of the continuity between Roman and Merovingian institutions and how much was passed on from the Merovingians to the Carolingians. A. Dopsch argued that for a long time there was little change in Roman institutions in Gaul, and economic and cultural life went on much as before. The rulers had changed, but everything else persisted. Even the new rulers continued to utilize without major changes the institutions they had inherited. Though few modern scholars would go as far as Dopsch today, part of the evidence that he adduced for his theory has been found acceptable. What present-day scholars would doubt is whether it adds up to as complete a continuity as he believed, although it is certainly enough to demonstrate that there was no sudden disruption of trade, and no wholesale replacement of Roman institutions and customs.

Henri Pirenne, an influential Belgian medievalist, many of whose pupils became leading medieval scholars in their turn, propounded an even more startling thesis—that the continuity of economic life inherited by the Merovingians from the Romans was maintained virtually intact until the rise of Islam and the Saracen conquest of the Mediterranean. The Mediterranean, according to Pirenne, remained the highway of commerce from Constantinople and the East, and the old Roman ports, such as Marseilles, retained their commercial importance. The money economy continued in operation. The Merovingians, in Pirenne's view, saw Italy as within their economic sphere; and Italy until the eighth century played a part not far different from its role during the Roman Empire, in spite of the change of rulers. All this comparative freedom of trade was disrupted, once and for all, by the Saracen victories in the Mediterranean and in Spain. The Germanic kingdoms thereafter began an economic decline, from which they began to emerge painfully only toward the end of the tenth and during the eleventh century. The new empire of Charlemagne, according to Pirenne, was henceforward cut off from the trade with the East that had been the lifeblood of the Roman and Merovingian world. It became landlocked, and thus was compelled to rely exclusively on its agricultural resources. Without Mahomet, Pirenne concluded, Charlemagne would have been "inconceivable."

It was a bold thesis, but it was never based solidly on fact. It rested rather on a somewhat arbitrary interpreta-

tion of a selected number of facts, and a neglect of others
inconvenient to the thesis. For example, it is true, as
Pirenne points out, that there were Eastern merchants in
Marseilles and elsewhere during the Merovingian era,
and that during the same period Egyptian papyrus was
still imported into Gaul. It is true also that gold coinage
was still in use, and had not yet been replaced by silver.
But R. Lopez and others have pointed out that the references to Syrian merchants in the work of Gregory of
Tours, who wrote in the sixth century, references relied
upon by Pirenne, are vague, and little of substance can
be inferred from them.

All the other evidence points to a decline of the quantity
and extent of the trade with the East during this period.
Such evidence as there is does not show any direct contact
between Merovingian Gaul and the Eastern Mediterranean. This trade, on the contrary, was with Africa
(Norman Baynes). Pirenne was unable to show that the
later abandonment of a gold coinage was due to a disruption of trade with Constantinople. Other reasons are
available to explain this abandonment.

What has been shown, however, and with conclusive
evidence, is that trade was never cut off at all by the
Saracens, who were, indeed, anxious to do as much
business with the West as they could. Neither the Saracens
nor the Jews and Syrians who formed the bulk of the
trading class had any ideological or religious objections to
this trade. Lastly, it should be emphasized that the Saracen
pirates did not win their limited mastery of the Mediterranean until long after the reign of Charlemagne.

Subsistence Economy of the Carolingian Epoch. The
truth appears to be that the undoubted decline of trade
from the time of the late Roman Empire, the final substitution of a silver for a gold currency, the paucity of
merchants in Western Europe in the time of Charlemagne,
and similar phenomena, need no complex hypothesis to
explain them. They are explainable simply by the fact
that the West had little to sell in eastern markets and so
was unable to buy more than a fraction of what it had
bought when there was a substantial industry in Western
Europe. The social and economic structure of Europe had
gradually changed over the centuries. The villa (large

estate) and the monastery were almost self-contained economic units. They consumed the vast bulk of what they produced, and they produced nothing of any quality that would find a market in eastern Europe or in Muslim lands. A few textiles were made in northern France and southern Frisia and taken abroad in Frisian ships. But there were few towns that were more than large villages, and almost no specialized industry of any kind. Pirenne, aware of this fact, suggested that the West exported slaves in exchange for eastern products. But though some slaves were certainly sent abroad, there is no evidence that bespeaks a heavy traffic in them.

The simple fact was that Europe had over the centuries sunk into a largely subsistence economy, and those who might have wished to consume had no products to exchange for the desired goods. Thus the trader could no longer make more than a bare living by buying and selling. Those merchants who did import could count on only a few customers who could afford to buy. What gold there was in Europe was quickly sent abroad and there was nothing to replace it. Thus a simple shortage of the most valuable metal made necessary a silver coinage for the minor transactions within Europe—and if papyrus, which in Egypt was cheaper than parchment, could not be imported for lack of the money to pay for it, then perforce parchment had to be used. At least it was available from western domestic sources, expensive though it was.

Both Pepin the Short and Charlemagne made serious efforts to stabilize the currency and substitute their own money for coins formerly casually minted by nobles. Eight hundred mints are known to have operated in Gaul during the seventh century. Although some gold coins were issued in the name of Charlemagne, for special purposes, the standard coin now became the silver denarius which weighed just over two grams. There was also an obol, half the value of the denarius. Under Charlemagne there were two hundred and forty denarii to the silver pound (livre) and twelve denarii to the gold solidus (sou). Charles recalled and forbade the circulation of money coined prior to his time, and throughout his reign tried to reduce the number of workshops where coins were minted, at one time confining it to his personal mint at Aachen. So little was money used, however, in the Carolingian age that neither the sou nor the livre was minted. They remained only as measures of value. The vast majority of the population fulfilled its obligations, including the payment of taxes, by contributions in kind.

For in the Carolingian society almost the whole production of the empire was drawn directly from the land. The typical unit was the great estate, the villa of the last days of the Roman Empire. Since the fall of Rome, the large estates had continued to grow, whether owned by great lords or by the Church. Small estates were still to be found, especially in eastern territories of the Frankish kingdom and empire, but they grew ever fewer in number as their owners voluntarily commended themselves to more powerful nobles who were better able to protect them in a dangerous epoch. We are able to learn much about these agricultural estates through the fortunate survival of an inventory, known as a *polyptic,* of the possessions and revenues of the French abbey of St. Germain des Prés. This polyptic dates from the Carolingian age. But of unique value to historians is the famous *Capitulare de villis,* issued by Charlemagne, or perhaps by his son Louis in his capacity as king of Aquitaine. This document is a detailed list of instructions as to what the monarch expected from the stewards on his estates. From such documents as these we have a very good idea of the manner in which the rural economy of the Carolingian epoch was organized.

The manors were divided into two parts—the demesne or home farm (*ager indominicatus*), the land set apart for the exclusive use of the lord; and the land held by the tenants. The former comprised from one sixth to one third of all the arable land—mostly as strips alongside the peasant strips, but sometimes as separate fields, the so-called close—plus vineyards, orchards, and a site for the manor house or castle. The land held by the tenants comprised the bulk of the arable land, together with pastures and meadows, forest and waste land. The tenants were organized as a village community. Though each individual villager or householder had a right to a holding of strips in the open fields (usually 30 acres each) the work, especially that on the lord's demesne, was the common responsibility of all the villagers. Originally the allotment of lands seems to have depended on the number of oxen a peasant could contribute to the common labor—one hide of 120 acres requiring eight oxen to cultivate.

Most of the tenants were theoretically free in status, but they were subject to so many restrictions on their freedom that they can hardly be distinguished from serfs. They were tied to their land and could not leave without the permission of their lords. In addition to these there were the true serfs or slaves, usually descended from slaves of the late Roman Empire. Some held tenancies from the lord, others were employed directly by him. In addition to work on the lord's fields, the tenants had to provide payments of money and in kind. Their wives and families were likewise required to provide various services for the lords. Any small industries such as bakeries, smithies, and such were manned by the tenants and their families. The women wove and sewed both in the lord's workshops and in their own homes for the lord and the lord's family, and provided domestic help in the lord's household. In the Carolingian age there was an absolute gulf fixed between the nobility, on the one side, and the peasants and workers, whether theoretically free or unfree.

Every estate was an independent, almost self-sufficient, economic entity. (*See especially Reading 10a, clause 42.*) The peasant had full security of tenure as long as he worked; but it was on his labor that the lord subsisted. The bulk of the peasantry, however, were not compelled to fight for the lords—though naturally in the event of an invasion their lands would not be spared the ravages of the enemy any more than the lands of their lords.

Fiscal Resources of the Monarchy. The Carolingian monarch was the chief landowner in the Empire, and he also laid claim to all land not settled and not in private possession. The *Capitulare de villis* (*see Reading No. 10a*) consists of royal instructions concerning the management of his estates and the income he expected from them. Each villa was under the control of a steward, who was himself responsible to a superintendent who looked after a number of royal estates. It was the steward who saw that the produce was taken to the royal barns and storehouses, and he was required to make an inventory of all he found on the estate (*see Reading No. 10*B), which he then submitted to the superintendent. The steward knew what was due to his master from every tenant, and he saw to it that the amount was paid, and it was he who arranged for the provision of the necessary numbers of artisans for the royal workshops. Charlemagne appears to have taken a personal interest in the efficiency of his stewards, and he was careful to see that the superintendents gave strict attention to their duties, and made a careful account of all the produce and money that they collected on his behalf.

The monarch did not have at his disposal any efficient tax-collecting system such as had existed in the later Roman Empire. He kept few paid officials and had little need of them. The foundation of the Carolingian fiscal system was the obligation of the monarch's subjects to make payments on certain definite occasions and for certain definite purposes—which occasions and purposes were well known to them. If the obligations were not met then the monarch had recourse to direct sanctions, especially the use of his courts of justice. He had so little means available to him for knowing what the resources were of his subjects that both income and property taxes were very difficult for him to assess. Although it would have been possible theoretically to impose taxes on the amount of land held, as had been the case in the Roman Empire, there is much evidence that such a tax was regarded by the landowners as "abusive." There are some capitularies which deal with direct property taxes, but it seems clear that such taxation had become very rare, and was enforceable only with so much difficulty that it had apparently fallen into virtual disuse.

The monarch, in fact, did not have very much need for actual money except for long wars. He needed money to support his own entourage and personal attendants, the upkeep of his places of residence, and the provision of a limited number of public works. He needed subsistence for himself and his followers while traveling and a few expensive luxuries which had to be imported. Most of these expenditures could be easily sustained from the revenues of his estates. For the rest the general principle in the

Carolingian age was that the local inhabitants had to provide what was needed on every occasion, and this was an obligation that they owed to the king personally as good subjects. When the king sent emissaries throughout the country on royal business, he did not provide them with traveling expenses. He gave them an order authorizing them to requisition what they needed from the lords of the territories through which they passed. The order specified in detail how many items were to be issued to them. These details varied according to the rank of the emissary. If a bridge had to be built, the obligation was laid upon the local authorities, and no cost to the monarch was involved.

The king, however, did have the right to certain customs and other indirect duties. The capitularies of the Carolingians make clear that such duties, which were collected at ports of entry, were to be exacted only for merchandise intended for sale. There were also duties collected on goods being transported within the kingdom in the form of tolls for use of certain bridges or roads. Finally, there were taxes on markets and fairs. In principle and by law all such tolls and duties were due only to the king. In later times they were either granted to or usurped by the local lords, who kept the proceeds for themselves when the monarchy was no longer strong enough to prevent it.

As has already been noted, a regular property tax was no longer collected by Charles, even though some capitularies refer to it as if it were still exacted. What appears to have taken its place was a "free gift," which was expected to be made to the monarch at the time of the annual May assembly. If such a gift were not made, the delinquent donor lost the favor of the king, with all that that entailed. (*See Reading No. 11*B.) There was no obligation for a definite amount, whether of money or of goods, though the gift was expected to be worthy of the position of the donor. Thus, although obligatory, the gift was not, in principle, a tax; it could not therefore be regarded as "abusive," as was a property tax. In theory it was a contribution to the monarch's expenses and a recognition of the services he performed for the benefit of all. Though the gift had, of course, ultimately to be paid by the peasants and tenants of the lord, who no doubt passed it on to them, it was an obligation clearly laid upon the great, rather than upon their poor retainers. The similarity of this "gift" to the taxation that was evolved in medieval England, under which the Parliaments "voted" taxes to the monarch, may be noted. Such English taxes were paid by the men who voted them, or, if they were able to pass them on, by their tenants and were regarded as a contribution to the king's expenses, especially in time of war. Otherwise the English king was expected to "live of his own." He could call on his subjects for "free contributions" only in time of special need. Likewise the French clergy paid *dons gratuits* to their monarch and were relieved of regular taxation right up to the French Revolution.

Lastly, it should be noted that substantial sums of money accrued to the royal treasury from the administration of justice. The monarch was entitled to his share of every fine imposed throughout the reign. Among these was the fine imposed on all those who failed to appear for their military service. (*See Reading No. 11A.*) The king's administrative officers, especially the counts, received their share of the proceeds of the courts of justice, which was no inconsiderable part of their income. In cases where laws had been broken and the fine was for a criminal offense, the count retained one third and remitted the remainder to the monarch. When a sum was assessed as damages to be paid to an individual, a third of the damages went to the Crown, and a third of this latter sum also to the count. Substantial sums might fall to the treasury in cases where punishment included confiscation of the possessions of the offender.

The only taxation that was based on income was the sacramental tithe (*decima*) which was due, not to the State, but to the Church. This practice, of course, has scriptural authority, and was inherited by the Christians from the Jews. Charlemagne, ever jealous for the Church, put the whole weight of his law and authority behind the Church in its efforts to collect the tithe, even from the newly converted peoples. He did not consider himself any more exempt than any of his subjects, since it was a religious duty to pay the tithe—though naturally some of the money thus received by the Church returned to him in the form of the "free gifts" made to him by the clergy. Charles also shared in any fines imposed on those who did not fulfill their ecclesiastical obligations and failed to pay the tithe.

The insistence of Charles on the payment of the tithe may be considered as part of the general tax system of the period. For lack of an imperial bureaucracy, all taxes had to be imposed directly on individuals and organizations capable of undertaking the onerous task, and many of the services performed by modern states had to be performed by private persons and the Church. To the Church fell the task of administering all that we think of today as social security. The abbey and the monastery were always open to the casual wayfarer. The Church undertook countless works of charity, in addition to providing religious solace and opening the path to salvation. Moreover almost the entire burden of education fell upon the Church. It was to Charles's interest to increase the ability of the Church to perform its tasks by endowing it with the necessary resources. Hence the extensive use of the privilege of immunity, originally applied to senatorial fiscal estates, by which the higher clergy were granted special rights and freedom from public taxation. In this way the Church was spared not only the taxes due to the monarch, but also any interference by judges or other royal officials. (*See Reading No. 13A*.) In return the Church provided the monarch with his sole source of literate helpers for the general administration of the realm.

Military Resources and Expenditures. The military expenses of Charles were regular and considerable. Military service was originally compulsory for all free men in the country, with the exception of minor clerics and monks and those who could provide a valid excuse. Abbots and bishops, however, were not excused. They were expected to go on campaign with the king, as well as to provide troops. Serfs were exempt. If any freeman "presumed to remain at home when the others go to war," he had to pay a large fine, called the *haribannus*. Deserters from the army might be condemned to death and the confiscation of all their property. (*See Reading No. 11A*.) In later times conscription was confined to landholders who held about 100 acres (four *mansi*) of land either as a freehold or as a benefice. (*See Reading No. 11c.*) It was the task of the local counts to assemble the ordinary troops and command them, while the king's own vassels joined him directly. The fighters had to come equipped fully at their own expense, and with sufficient rations for three months. The arms that had to be supplied by each warrior were carefully prescribed, and fines were imposed on those who did not bring their quota. In addition to rations clothes, arms, and material, which included tools such as hatchets and pickaxes, had to be brought, including wagons to carry them. These supplementary items were supposed to be sufficient to last for six months.

The decision to initiate a campaign was taken by the monarch himself. In theory he had to take the advice of a General Assembly, known as the Fields of May.* (*See Reading No. 11b.*) But in fact, approval of the king's projects was a foregone conclusion, and the troops, who had already assembled for the purpose of going to war, were never sent home without fighting. Hardly a year went by without the call for war, and often there were several wars in progress at the same time.

Yet, it is also true that very seldom were all the troops called out who were legally liable for service, and the campaigns themselves were short. They usually began in July or August and lasted only two or three months. The monarch, it is true, had the right to demand a longer term of service. But he did not often exact it, since he would then himself be required to provide food for his troops after their three months' supply was exhausted. Sometimes it was necessary, as, for example, in Charles's last campaign against the Lombard king Desiderius, but such occasions were rare. The troops were never permitted to live off the countryside through which they passed, though in enemy country some booty might be expected in which they could share.

It can hardly be questioned that military service was

* At one time the Frankish General Assembly had been called in March, but in March there was insufficient fodder available for the horses. When the king began to place greater reliance on his cavalry, the Assembly date was changed to May.

the most costly and onerous of the duties that had to be performed by the subjects of Charlemagne. The system, however, provided the monarch with the means for extending his empire at relatively low cost to himself, and he did not need to be a military or administrative genius to be able to put into the field far more troops than could ever be massed against him by any adversary he was at all likely to encounter in his age.

Administration of the Carolingian Realm: The Monarch. To understand the means by which Charles maintained his civil government it is always necessary to remember that he was compelled to make use of the human and institutional resources that he inherited and that there were certain physical limits imposed on him by conditions of the time which he was powerless to change. Among the latter must be counted the extremely primitive means of communication between one part of his empire and another. The old Roman roads along which the Roman legions had marched to the frontiers had been allowed to fall into decay, and even the remnants of the Roman roads were not available in the eastern part of Charles's dominions. Large tracts of forest and marshlands, unfordable rivers, to say nothing of mountains, disrupted communications. Nothing was available to Charles like the great roads built by the ancient Persians in their huge empire, nor the relay system of royal couriers.

In some respects the Carolingian imperial system resembles that of Persia in the fifth century B.C. The Persian satraps resemble the Carolingian counts, and the so-called "eyes and ears" of the Persian monarch, whose task was to keep the king informed of everything that went on in his realm, including the activities of the satraps, resemble nothing in the West so much as the Carolingian *missi dominici*. The comparison should not be carried too far, for the Frankish ruler and his people were incomparably more barbarous than the ancient Persians, or at least than the Persian upper classes who administered the realm for the monarch.

In an almost wholly illiterate society such as the Carolingian empire, in which warfare was a constant fact of life, and in which an aristocracy flourished that was always ready to rebel against a monarch who failed to respect its hereditary rights, there was a limit beyond which no single ruler could go. Even if Charles had been succeeded by others as able and devoted as himself and had bequeathed to them intact all that he had himself inherited and won, this society could not have been fundamentally changed. All that Charles could hope to do was to impose his own will on those with whom he had to work, maintain the existing laws and customs of his realm, and establish his own as the final authority beyond which there could be no appeal. What he aimed at, and in large measure accomplished, was to establish a safe and orderly kingdom, put bounds to the power of the nobles, and see that justice was maintained.

The heart of the entire Carolingian regime was the person of the monarch himself. The General Assembly or Field of May met annually to give him advice on any subjects he laid before it, and it gave him advice when he asked for it. It even ratified the position of the monarch when he ascended the throne. But it was no real check on his power. It was simply an advisory body, to which in his wisdom the monarch gave attention, and whose views he incorporated in his capitularies, when he desired to do so. But he did not have to wait for the Field of May before promulgating the capitularies. He could and did issue them at any time, and merely informed the Assembly when next it met.

Though absolute, the monarch was not arbitrary. Though he was the supreme legislator, he was, nevertheless, bound by the laws, whether of his own making or the traditional laws and customs of the people of his realm. Though responsible to no man, he believed himself responsible to God, and he tried to take this responsibility seriously. All men in his realm owed fidelity to him. He required all his free subjects to take a personal oath of fidelity to him, which oath they renewed when he became emperor. Indeed, so important was this oath to Charles that in 802 he gave special instructions to his *missi* to impose it on all freemen, down to the twelve-year-olds. (*See Reading No. 12, ch. 2.*) This oath was far more than a simple pledge to be faithful. It included an oath of absolute obedience that was unqualified, whatever the monarch might demand. It included a promise to obey all the laws of the land, to pay taxes on demand, not to damage the land, nor in any way to injure the Church. Anyone who failed to live up to his oath of fidelity was thus guilty not only of an ordinary crime against the state, but of perjury—a far more heinous offense in an age when oaths were truly believed to be sacred. This oath of fidelity was taken directly to the monarch by the great nobles of the realm; the other freemen took it to the local count or to the *missi* as the king's representatives.

The Royal Household. In all Germanic countries the king's household was the center of power—in this differing from the Roman or Byzantine empire, where an impersonal bureaucracy might share power with the ruler. Though the officers of the household were, before all else, the personal attendants of the monarch, they also had numerous administrative tasks to perform. The four great household offices were those of seneschal, butler, marshal, and chamberlain. The chief position was that of the chamberlain (*camerarius*), one of whose tasks was to guard the king's chamber, where the royal treasure was deposited. Although the old title of "mayor of the palace" had disappeared with the elevation to the kingship of Pepin the Short, the last mayor, many of the functions of the former mayor fell to the new chamberlain. His official task was to supervise all branches of the royal household. This included such matters as the dispensing of the king's charity, giving him counsel, and occasionally rendering judgment for him.

Almost equal in honor, if not in power, were the seneschal and butler whose task was to provide the royal household with food and drink. The marshal, or constable, supervised the royal stables. To the strictly "domestic" functions of these men were added other important nondomestic duties, as in the case of the chamberlain. The holders of all these offices were invariably nobles, and they were the closest counselors to the monarch in the Carolingian age and for centuries thereafter.

Last among the lay officials should be mentioned the "counts of the palace" (counts palatine), who supervised the administration of justice in the name of the monarch, and presided over the royal tribunal when the monarch could not be present in person. These men also were leading members of the aristocracy.

The king had at his disposal a personal chaplain (*capellanus*), a senior cleric whom Charles persuaded the pope to grant the title of archbishop, in spite of the fact that he did not preside over an archbishopric. He did, however, possess a bishopric and the emoluments that went with it. But he was not required to live in and administer the work of his diocese. This man was the king's personal adviser on ecclesiastical matters and corresponds in some degree to the position of the English archbishop of Canterbury under the Norman kings. This official, of course, was appointed by the monarch, though his ecclesiastical title was conferred on him by the pope. One text refers to the chaplain as the "archbishop of the sacred palace," and gives him precedence over other archbishops of the empire.

The only bureaucratic and specialized institution of the imperial government was the chancery, which had already existed under the Merovingian kings and mayors, but was given greater importance by Pepin and Charles. The *referendarii* of Merovingian times had been lay officials. They were now replaced by ecclesiastics who as such were attached and subordinated to the chaplain (later archchaplain) of the palace. The clerks and notaries of the chancery were in charge of drafting, registering, and storing royal documents. Charles selected as heads of the chancery persons of high rank and quality, and rewarded their services with high ecclesiastical positions. Charles's son and grandsons conferred special titles upon them. Among these the one that came into general use was that of chancellor (*cancellarius*).

Imperial Control and Administration. The key to the organization of the Carolingian empire was the system of counties (*pagus, Gau*), each headed by a count (*Graf*). There were several hundred such counties, some hardly larger than a New England township though others were as immense as some counties in the American West. It was Charles's custom to appoint as head of a county a nobleman, who was his personal representative in the area. He was judge, police officer, and commanded the soldiers of his *pagus* in war. Under him were *centenarii*, or vicars, who headed the hundreds (*centenae*). If the territory was large and the work too great for the count to handle, he had the right to appoint an assistant called a viscount, whose appointment had to be confirmed by the monarch. Some of the smaller counties in the time of Charlemagne had only viscounts at their head. But they were in the first instance responsible to the counts, who would in this case be entrusted by the king with several counties. In theory the counts held office only during the monarch's pleasure and could be transferred from one county to another. In practice the counts held office for considerable periods of time, and their offices would sometimes be taken over by their sons.

For all this there were Merovingian precedents, as recounted in Chapter 1. The Frankish dukes appointed as Merovingian viceroys in the outlying Frankish territories gradually shook off the ties which bound them to the monarchs and became virtually independent. The Carolingian counts were not paid salaries. Their means of subsistence was provided by a *beneficium*, a grant of land that accompanied the office. This land, of which it was difficult to dispossess them, likewise became the permanent property of themselves and their descendants, together with the office for which the land had originally been granted.

Some of the counts were given military responsibility also in certain frontier areas. These were organized by Charles as centers for defense and expansion into the neighboring pagan lands. In these marches, as they were called, there was one super-count known as count of the march (*Markgraf, margrave*), who could command the services of the ordinary counts in his area. Such men naturally had the duty of summoning troops needed to defend the frontier committed to their charge. All counts had their courts, administering justice on the king's behalf; to them the monarch dispatched his instructions in the form of capitularies. In every respect they acted as the king's representatives; and it was not at all surprising that they were often the first to throw off the royal authority when it began to weaken after the death of Charlemagne.

The count was the chief lay authority in the territories

which he administered. But most counties were of much the same size as the episcopal dioceses. These dioceses were ruled by the bishop in all ecclesiastical matters. Since the bishops were appointed by the monarch, the latter regarded them as his servants in much the same way as he regarded the counts—and in some instances bishops themselves were indeed granted the privileges and duties of counts. In the Carolingian age bishops had hardly less authority than counts in the affairs that concerned them. The bishops, however, were not subject to the authority of the counts. Both bishops and counts were responsible only to the monarch and to the emissaries of the monarch who visited their territories on his behalf.

In Charles's day it was impossible for counts to throw off the yoke of the monarch, even had they wished it. Not only had the latter too much power at his disposal from his other territories which could be brought to bear on any rebel, but he also kept a close supervision on their behavior and actions. The means of supervision was the system of royal emissaries (*missi dominici*) instituted by Charlemagne. Two men, one of whom was a count and one a cleric, usually a bishop but sometimes an abbot, were armed with royal authority and sent on a tour of inspection to a specific district. Their task was to see that the count in the area was keeping the peace, maintaining the king's justice, remitting the proper dues to the monarch, assisting the Church, and in general administering the territory with efficiency. Many of the commissions given to these *missi* are extant, from which it may be seen what wide powers they were granted and how many aspects of administration, both secular and ecclesiastical, they had to examine—ranging from restoring fugitive royal serfs to their servitude and seeing that no one poached game illegally in the emperor's forests, to overseeing the behavior of monks in their monasteries. (*See Reading No. 12, chs. 4, 39.*) The free men of the county were entitled to bring any complaints to the *missi* for investigation; the *missi* on their own authority and in the emperor's name were instructed to inquire into any arbitrary behavior or injustice committed by the count. They were also instructed to hear lawsuits and to summon meetings or inquests to inquire into whether any crimes had been committed in the area. Thus, via Flanders and Normandy, they provided a prototype for the itinerant justices sent out in England in the early twelfth century, which developed into the assizes still held today in Great Britain.

Naturally, the authority of the *missi* was no greater than that of their master. The later Carolingians continued to make use of the system as long as they could. But while Charles in the later part of his reign sent out his *missi* on as many as four missions in the year, so that some counts who went on missions could spend little time in their own counties, making necessary the appointment of viscounts, the later Carolingians too often allowed counts to supervise their own areas and those contiguous to them, thus largely defeating the purposes of the system. Moreover, it was of little value to authorize visits if the monarchs themselves, unlike Charlemagne, were not in a position to redress any grievances or dismiss counts who had been found to be derelict in their duties. But during the reign of Charles the reports of the *missi* were invaluable to him as sources of information as to what was being done in his name in his territories, and to enable him to keep effective control of all parts of his empire.

It should be noted that there were some variations in the administrative arrangements in the different parts of the empire. Not all of the territories were peopled by Franks, and not all had submitted gracefully to Frankish rule when it had been imposed on them. Charlemagne was well aware of the particularism of the separate entities. The *missi* system enabled him to confer a different status on some parts of his realm, while retaining as effective control in his own hands as if they had been Frankish.

In Aquitaine, for example, where Charles had had his son crowned king with his own court and officials, the *missi* reported in exactly the same manner as in the other provinces ruled directly by Charles himself. A similar situation obtained in Bavaria, where Charles appointed his brother-in-law governor, and in Lombardy, given to his son Pepin to rule. Even in some of the former Byzantine territories in Italy which had been handed over to the pope, Charles exercised some authority as *patricius,* and in spite of the formal objections of the pope he sent his *missi* there, as he did to Istria, which was put in the charge of a duke to replace the former Byzantine official.

It will be clear from the foregoing that Charles believed in centralized control of his empire in so far as this was feasible in his day. He made regulations for the administration and took steps to see that they were carried out by his appointees, who were not necessarily local men. They were chosen from such members of the aristocracy as were available, and they could be stationed wherever the emperor desired, and transferred at his will. They were compelled by their oath of fidelity to obey him; if they disobeyed they could be deprived of the land that accompanied their appointment. It was not, however, too easy to transfer them, since the land they were granted was their sole means of subsistence, aside from their share of the fines they imposed in their courts of justice. Thus they tended to acquire a vested interest in their position and lands, as we have seen; and when the reins of imperial control were loosened, it became very difficult indeed to dislodge them. By this time also they had acquired some local patriotism, enabling them to command support in their counties from men who no doubt felt themselves to be at least as much his subjects as subjects of the distant emperor.

The Carolingian system, therefore, held within itself the seeds of its own decay. The centrifugal forces were far stronger than the forces making for integration. When Charles was dead, wars between the rulers of the separate divisions of the empire, and invasions from outside, would play into the hands of the local landowners and increase their power at the expense of the center. Before the end of the ninth century the beginnings of the separate kingdoms of the Middle Ages could already have been discerned, to say nothing of the feudal fragmentations of these kingdoms.

It was a process that, to the historian's eye, could hardly have been avoided. The great empire of Charlemagne was a brilliant interlude, a jerry-built edifice held together by the ability, energy, and personality of the emperor; but with no future in its own right—even though in its decay it helped to mold the whole future of Europe as it was to become in later ages.

Administration of Justice. Centralizer though he was

within limits, Charles did not possess the means, even if he had had the will, to change in any radical manner the traditions and customs of the empire. The Romans had imposed their superior law upon their empire, and in time their subjects had fully accepted it. Thus Roman law, like Roman administration, was a unifying and civilizing influence upon the peoples of the empire. It was essentially territorial law. In the Frankish kingdom there was no such universal law. Each people had the right to "confess" its own law, whether German or Roman. Descendants of Romans had the right to be tried by any of the various codified forms of Roman law. Each member of the old German tribes—Lombard, Burgundian, Salian, Ripuarian, Frank, Alemannian, Bavarian, or any other—could likewise be tried under his own laws. Unwritten laws, for example the Bavarian and Ripuarian laws, were codified by Charlemagne in Latin for the first time. Others like the *Lex Salica* were edited authoritatively. All these were customary and tribal laws (*Leges barbarorum*), concerned with such matters as the composition money (*wergeld*) for murder, fines for various offenses, judicial procedure, treason, and in general the violation of the king's peace. According to Germanic legal theory, Charles could make no new laws, but could add to the customs of his peoples by capitularies and ordinances (*legibus addenda*—"additions" to the law), which, however, had to be approved formally by the assembly of magnates. In judging cases the count, who might be quite unfamiliar with the law under which a defendant was to be tried, was assisted by local assessors, who helped him to arrive at a judgment and assess a suitable penalty.

What Charles, always aware of his role as the supreme fount of justice in his dominions, did was to institute a procedure for lawsuits which varied as little as possible from one end of the empire to the other. In pre-Carolingian days the assessors who assisted the counts, vicars, or viscounts had been chosen from local notables. Charles's principal reform was to institute a special permanent college of assessors (*scabini, échevins, Schöffen* in the north, *iudices* in the south) in each county, appointed and supervised by a count, instead of the casual nonprofessional assessors of his predecessors. These assessors were twelve in number, seven of whom constituted a quorum. In earlier time all freemen were required to be present at the court sessions, which was a heavy burden to them. Charles seems to have limited their compulsory attendance to three regular sessions (unbidden, *ungebotene thinge*). For the irregular sessions (bidden, *gebotene thinge*) only the parties to a suit were summoned. Such a procedure was made possible only by the presence of the *scabini,* whose expert advice replaced the general (but inexpert) opinion of the whole body of freemen. Only freemen were entitled to the protection of the king's justice.

In an ordinary private suit there would naturally be two parties involved, the complainant and the defendant. There was no formal public prosecutor for cases where there was no private complainant. But the count, being required to maintain law and order in his territories, and entitled to receive a third of the fines imposed, would naturally have an interest in certain cases. In particular, it was his duty to prosecute in cases of disturbance of the public order. Royal capitularies specified the kinds of crimes the count should take it upon himself to punish. The sentences meted out by his court were subject to appeal to the *missi* when they were on their tours of inspection. As noted earlier, the latter had the right to institute cases where the count was believed to have been lax in his duties. The *missi* were instructed to hold four assizes in different localities in each county, and they too were assisted by the college of assessors. The *missi* had the right to reserve cases for the decision of the monarch himself—which in practice, save in very exceptional cases, would mean decisions by the royal tribunal presided over by one of the counts palatine. This court was made up of notables of the royal household rather than professional assessors. The defendant might also appeal to the royal court if he believed that his case had been wrongly judged. Finally, a few cases were reserved for the royal court, especially those in which a count or a large landholder or a high official of the Church was involved.

Little need be said here on the functioning of the ecclesiastical courts which had jurisdiction in matters concerning the Church and religious affairs, and were presided over by the bishop or his nominee. Appeals to the

royal court were permitted also from ecclesiastical judg-
ments. This, of course, was in full accord with the emperor's role as conceived by himself. It was his responsibility before God to see that the Church fulfilled its own
task, that it judged in accordance with right and equity,
that it maintained the purity of the Christian faith. The
officials of the Church were responsible to him as much
as or more than they were responsible to their own ecclesiastical superiors. Charles chose them for their offices, and
he could discipline them. He never deviated from his
belief that there was nothing that was done in his realm
that did not concern him, that he was chosen by God, and
responsible to God alone for the charge entrusted to him.

"Happy is the people," Alcuin once wrote in the fervor
of his admiration for his royal master, "exalted by a chief
and supported by a preacher of the faith, whose right
hand brandishes the triumphal sword, and whose mouth
makes the trumpet of Catholic truth resound. So once
David, chosen by God as king of the people which was
then his chosen people, subdued foreign nations by his
victorious sword, and preached the divine law among his
people." *

**Social Changes: The Disintegration of the Freeman
Class.** In the generally bright picture of Charles's reign,
dark colors are not lacking. During his lifetime and beyond, the empire enjoyed a measure of economic prosperity. But there is enough evidence to indicate that during the period conditions were rapidly deteriorating for
the minor freemen who still held their own property
(*allod*). Most of them were compelled either by economic
disasters or by pressure from the rich landowners to give
up their property to these men and to accept the servile
obligations entailed by such a surrender. At the same time
the domains of ecclesiastical and secular lords were in-
creasing not only through their acquisition of small properties but by lavish grants made to them by the monarch.

Yet it is not simply the familiar story of the rich growing richer while the poor grew poorer. Wealth entailed
power, as always; but in this period the growing power
of the landowners meant the replacement of public authority and law by law imposed by local magnates on

* Alcuin, *Letters,* II, 41.

economically dependent people. Efforts made by the central government to protect the poor proved futile. Indeed, the government itself contributed to the process in various ways, especially by the encouragement it gave to the formation of feudal ties between the great landowners and groups of freemen eager to associate themselves with lords in exchange for services which tended to raise rather than lower their social status—anything, in fact, short of menial work. The rise of a class of "vassals" bound to magnates by personal and material ties greatly helped the efforts of the magnates to shake off the authority of the monarch and to superimpose their economic and juridical authority on an ever-growing number of bondsmen.

It is true that the emperor had reserved for himself the right to appoint all local officials, counts, dukes, margraves, and their subordinates and had exercised a strict supervision over their work through the visits of the *missi*. But, as a result of the weakening of the monarchy after the death of Charles, these local officials bequeathed their positions to their sons together with the land and revenues that went with them. Thus the former administrative districts of the empire were removed from central control and converted into independently ruled political divisions. The process involved not only the complete loss of all central control over the ruling families by the king—later to be replaced by feudal suzerainty, the weakest of contractual bonds—but also over the population in these areas. Long before the Carolingian era these conditions had found legal (royal) sanction in the immunities. (*See Reading No. 13A.*)

Instead of the earlier ruler-subject relationship there thus grew up a relationship based on personal loyalty and land tenure, which could be effective only within a small group and in limited areas. So the fragmentation resulting from the process was greater even than that entailed by the detachment of the larger administrative units from the central government. The centrifugal forces, therefore, already to be observed in operation before the Carolingian era, became more institutionalized during this period. The result was the localism and fragmentation of government characteristic of the Middle Ages, with its innumerable regions of varying size and its overlapping jurisdictions in the hands of thousands of more or less independent local lords.

As early as Merovingian times magnates had been eager to form their own military retinue on the model of the royal *trustis*. This royal bodyguard bound to the king only by the oath of fidelity—a direct succession to the German *comitatus*—constituted part of the royal power. In course of time the groups from which both the king and the magnates drew their retainers widened, to include freedmen, or men who had commended themselves in exchange for protection and maintenance (clients, *vassi*). (*See Reading No. 13B.*) These clients were encouraged to perform military service for their lords and were given land to enable them to equip themselves in accordance with the lords' wishes. The Church likewise availed itself of the immense tracts of land granted to it by pious Christians for the care of their souls. The Church was thus enabled to fulfill its obligation to provide armed men for the king's army. The term that now came into use for land granted in return for military service was benefice (*beneficium*). The "beneficiary" was bound to the lord by the same oath of fidelity that in earlier times had bound the member of the *trustis* or *comitatus* to his leader. This raised the status of the former *vassus* to that of the aristocracy of fighters; they were to become the vassals of the medieval feudal system—sharing with the landed aristocracy the privilege of being treated as "freemen," that is, to be tried by their own "personal" law, with all the social prestige attached to it.

The process was hastened by military necessity. When Charles Martel needed a large cavalry corps to meet the danger of Saracen invasion, he granted "benefices" to prospective cavalrymen large enough to cover the costs of this particularly expensive military service. When he had nearly exhausted the royal estates and his own he confiscated land of the Church for the same purpose. Land thus held by benefice from the Church was later called land "borrowed" by order of the king (*precarium verbo regis*). The Frankish magnates were encouraged to give out their own land as benefices for the purpose of endowing a fighting force.

The rulers, especially Charlemagne, did not perceive

that this process diminished their power. On the contrary, they considered that the close ties established between a local leader and his fighting men improved the efficiency and discipline of their armies. A man fighting under the eyes of his immediate overlord would be especially anxious not to damage his reputation by cowardice or neglect of duty. Charlemagne, indeed, exhorted the freeman to "come with his lord, if the lord goes, or with his count." (*See Reading No. 11c.*) He also commanded the counts to come to the assembly preceding each campaign together with their "men," their own vassals, and those of the king who lived in their counties. In later times, and for the same reason (847), the later Carolingians instructed each man to "choose a lord." (*See Reading No. 13c.*) Thus the rise of a fighting aristocracy constituted a part of the historical process of expanding the Carolingian empire.

    The Lesser Freeman and the Serf. Although the Carolingian period was, on the whole, a prosperous one, there are signs of economic exhaustion on the part of large masses of the people, coupled with a struggle on the part of the magnates for "their share in the shrinking resources which were no longer sufficient for all" (H. Fichtenau). There had always been famines—the famine of 791 had in some places led to cannibalism—and they were followed by plagues. The most alarming sign of this economic deterioration, as far as Charles's government was concerned, was the plight of "the poor," the small landholder whose property had diminished or dwindled away and who lost his freedom because he had surrendered "to the power of potentates." Charles had diligent enquiries made "into these conditions and their causes." While his government knew no cure for natural disasters other than resorting to prayer and appealing to the spirit of charity among the great, he did try, albeit vainly, to prevent the magnates from pressing the poor into surrendering their estates. It was thought that this tendency was solely responsible for the evils which ensued, including the diminution of services to the government, the flight to the monasteries, and the disinheriting of a whole class of freemen "forced by want to become robbers and criminals." (*See Readings Nos. 13d to 13f.*)

The plight of those who surrendered was indeed a hard one. In St. Germain des Prés "free" tenants had to perform five weeks of labor in the year, whereas those whose status became similar to that of the *coloni* in the western part of the empire had to accept "unfree" tenure, with the heavy sacrifices that this status entailed. Although the exploitation of the poor was a conventional topic for sermons, it is clear from the measures taken to prevent serfs from running away that there was some truth in it. Indeed, serfs escaped so often that an astrological calendar of the period recommends certain days as those most favorable for such escapes.

The greed of the nobles, however, is only a part of the story. The surrender of the *allod* to rich landowners was often a voluntary act, contracted for by the parties involved. The surrender of an *allod* to a lord, and receiving it back as a *precarium* gave the poor man certain advantages in an age of expanding empire when he was required to serve in regular annual campaigns and to perform other public duties. The surrender did not of course free him from all military duties, but his lord bore some of the economic burden and was even able to buy his release from public building services due to the king.

In his later years Charles himself speeded this development. Seeing that society was suffering from serious food shortages and that the lesser landowners found it impossible to make a living for themselves and their families while struggling at the same time to cope with their military obligations, he introduced a quota system in various regions of his empire. Royal capitularies distinguished between rich and poor landowners, permitting the peasants to devote themselves to farming while paying for the equipment of one man who would go to war in their stead. (*See Reading No. 11c.*) This arrangement contributed to the division of society into a class of warriors and a class of toilers. The lesser landowners who undertook the military burden, although not initially of a different class from other landowners, now became specialized as fighters, with a higher status than their former peers, who became hardly distinguishable from peasants. This division of society, characteristic of the Middle Ages, was hastened by the Carolingians and their imperial necessities.

CHURCH AND STATE IN THE CAROLINGIAN AGE

Reorganization of the Church under Charles Martel and Pepin the Short. The Merovingian age had seen the Church almost completely secularized and religious life degraded and neglected. Too often the highest positions in the Church were held by men who were wholly unsuited for them—even by laymen, who were usually chosen from the court circle and consecrated without any religious preparation. Charles Martel may have desired to institute reforms in his Frankish territories, but he was so fully absorbed in his wars that he could not give any major part of his attention to it. Indeed, he contributed in some measure to the further decline of the Frankish Church when he sequestrated Church lands, thus depriving it of much needed revenues, bestowing them on the magnates to enable them to provide him with cavalrymen for his wars. Charles, however, did give some support to missionary enterprise among the pagans, especially to the work of St. Boniface.

This remarkable man, an English priest born in Wessex about 675 and baptized under the name of Winfred, was both a missionary to the pagans and a great Church reformer. He had studied under the famous scholar Aldhelm and taught in an English monastery (Nursling, near Southampton) until he was forty years of age. Only then did he move out into the world and undertake the prodigious labors on behalf of the Church which earned him the title of "Apostle of Germany" and the position of archbishop and papal legate in Frankland.

The great impetus toward the reawakening of religious life in Gaul and Germany had come from the monasteries of Ireland with the arrival of St. Columban and his companions on the continent of Europe about 585. This promising missionary work was continued by an Englishman,

St. Willibrord, who had studied in Ireland and whose companions included many Irishmen. St. Willibrord worked
especially in Frisia. The great centers of piety, asceticism,
and learning in the seventh and early eighth centuries were
in Ireland and England, at the very time when the Church
in Merovingian Gaul was reaching its lowest depths of
degradation. Moreover, the Anglo-Saxon Church had been
very systematically organized by Rome in the seventh
century. For this reason the Anglo-Saxons believed very
strongly in the necessity of always working with papal
support and in the efficiency of the typically Roman hier-
archical form of organization. This preference, together
with his Anglo Saxon connections (see Readings Nos. 14A
and 14B), did not endear Boniface to the Frankish clergy,
who frequently opposed him when his work impinged on
their prerogatives and more particularly when he was
granted the authority to continue his reforms in the Frankish heartland.

Boniface's first mission was to the Frisians (716),
where he did his best to aid St. Willibrord. But the difficulties were such that he soon returned to England. In
719 he visited Rome, where Pope Gregory II gave him
his Roman name of Boniface and blessed his mission. He
then began his missionary work among the Hessians and
later the Thuringians. In 722 he was made bishop by
Pope Gregory II, and it was on this occasion that he took
an oath to the pope "to show in all things a perfect loyalty to you and to the welfare of the Church." He also
promised to attempt to discipline any bishops who were
"opponents of the ancient institutions of the Holy Fathers." (See Reading No. 14C.) In fact Boniface did meet
with opposition from the bishop of Mainz, who strongly
objected to his mission, which he appears to have regarded
as unwarranted interference by a foreigner, even though
he held his commission from the pope. It was a great
comfort for Boniface, therefore, that he could refer to
Rome in all the difficulties which he encountered in his
dealing with the Frankish clergy as well as in his mission.
(See Reading No. 14D.)

In 732 Boniface was made archbishop. Before his work
was quite finished in Thuringia Pope Gregory III sent him
to Bavaria and Alemannia. But the latter province was

already in the capable hands of Bishop Pirmin, who was most probably a refugee from Visigoth Spain and who, under the protection of Charles Martel, founded several monasteries, among them the famous Reichenau. Boniface, for his part, was extremely successful in Bavaria. His work was confirmed and approved by the pope in 739. (*See Reading No. 14*E.)

During all this time Charles Martel had given some support to Boniface as to the other missions that were in operation, and Boniface admitted that he could not have been successful without his aid. When Charles died in 741, to be succeeded by his two sons as mayors of the palace, the reform of the clergy that had been a feature of Boniface's missionary work outside the Frankish heartland had not yet been undertaken within it. This was now to change, since both Carloman, the mayor of Austrasia, and Pepin, mayor of Neustria, felt it part of their office to abolish abuses, but seemed also stirred by the desire to win the help of St. Peter through his delegate, the apostle Boniface. In 742 Carloman called a synod, the first such synod to be held during the eighth century, for the purpose, as he stated it, of reëstablishing the laws of the Church and purifying the Christian religion. The synod started its work by confirming the missionary bishops established by Boniface "for the several cities" and by setting him over them as archbishop. (*See Reading No. 14*F.) In a second synod (743), among other matters, Carloman promised to restore part of the lands taken from the Church by Charles Martel (*see the same Reading*) as did Pepin in his own synod of 744. This promise neither he nor Pepin was able to carry out, but promises to make regular payments as partial compensation were better observed. Charlemagne modified the arrangements of his predecessors in 779. (*See Reading No. 14*H.)*

In 744 Pepin called a synod of his own, but he en-

---

* The men who had received benefices from Church land *precario verbo regis* were required by the Carolingians to pay special taxes known as "the tenth and the ninth" (*decima et nona*), to be distinguished from the universal sacramental tithe. The tithe was paid to the parish priest, whereas "the tenth and ninth" went to the Church that had been deprived of the land for the "beneficiary."

countered more obstinate opposition from the Neustrian bishops than had been met with by his brother. The bishops objected to a centralized organization of the Church and evidently feared for their prerogatives. It would appear from the sequel in the next years that Pepin decided to go slow with the centralizing of the control of the higher clergy in his territories, concentrating on other reforms which were more easily carried out. The celibacy of the higher clergy was enforced, and the annual visitations of the bishops in their dioceses were regularized. When Carloman abdicated in 747 and went into a monastery, Pepin became mayor of the whole realm ruled by his father, and in the next few years Boniface appears to have been strongly dissatisfied with the progress of the reform. Though devoting much of his time to his newly founded abbey of Fulda he certainly encountered opposition from the Frankish clergy. The pope clearly continued to back him, but it may be that Pepin's zeal had indeed cooled by this time, and Boniface's complaints had some substance.

Pepin himself, however, was still in need of papal support, since he was planning to put aside the last titular Merovingian ruler of his territories and become king himself. When Pope Zacharias in 751 approved this step it was Boniface, as the leading churchman in the country, who was deputed to anoint him.* But soon afterward the aged prelate left the country for ever, eventually meeting his end in Frisia, where he was murdered by pagans who still refused in spite of all the missions to their country, to accept Christianity.

From the time he became king and after Boniface's death Pepin was free to go his own way in ecclesiastical policy. There was no break in any respect with the papacy, which was now in greater need of Pepin's support than he was in need of the papacy. But the subordination of the bishops to the Roman Church, which had been a feature of Boniface's program, was quietly dropped. Pepin had the bishop of Metz made metropolitan with leadership over the Austrasian Church, and at that time Boniface's successor did not become metropolitan of Mainz,

* It is still not entirely certain that it was Boniface who anointed Pepin, but the belief that it was he has been long hallowed by tradition.

as Boniface himself had been. It is possible that the Frankish clergy were trying to rid their Church of Anglo-Saxon
influence, and that they had opposed Boniface in part because he was an Anglo-Saxon.

On the other hand, Pepin and the Frankish clergy did
not allow the reform work of Boniface to lapse altogether.
In 755 the king called a synod of the Frankish clergy
whose decisions he later published in the form of a capitulary. The synod decided to abolish immediately the most
harmful abuses. Church discipline was to be restored and
the bishops were made responsible for the ecclesiastical
matters in their respective *parrochia*. Some of them were
appointed to act as metropolitans until the time when it
would be possible to restore the metropolitan organization
in its entirety "according to canonical institutions." (*See
Reading No. 14*G.) From this synod and those that followed it becomes quite clear that the king was, and desired to remain, master in his own house. The ideal of
Boniface, an ideal which he tried to put in effect at Fulda,
which was independent and in direct relations to Rome,
was not possible under the system of a Frankish territorial
Church. On the other hand, Bonifaces's endeavors
to link the Frankish Church to Rome were not altogether
lost. Owing to his influence the Carolingians brought ecclesiastical matters as well as matters of public and private
morality in line with canon law, the practice of the Roman
see. In all his institutions, whether they concerned the behavior of the clergy or the life of the people in such matters as marriage, Pepin tried to restore "the ancient canons
of the fathers." The same can be said about his son
Charles. To assess the reform work of the eighth century
in the words of W. Levison, "the result was not an unlim-
ited influence of the pope on the Frankish Church, for the
king remained its ruler; but the connection with Rome
became much stronger and more effective than before
though it also included problems of conflict which later
times had to face."

Charlemagne and the Church. One of Charles's most
important contributions to the reform work initiated by
Boniface was the completion of the provincial and metropolitan organization of the Frankish Church. In the course
of his reign all the old metropolitan provinces with their

sees were reëstablished; the dignity of an archbishop was now definitely attached to the sees of Cologne and Mainz with authority over the newly organized dioceses in Saxony; and a new see was created in Salzburg for the Bavarian province in which newly conquered Pannonia was incorporated. In Mainz Boniface's chief disciple and successor Lullus was finally made archbishop and received the pallium. Charles also recognized the right of the pope to confer the pallium upon the archbishops as evidence of their special function. The king devoted a great part of his legislation to the reform of the Church—for instance, to the strengthening of the authority of the bishops in their dioceses and the restoration of discipline among the clergy. These decrees were usually the result of the policy adopted at the synods, which by now were "a relatively regular feature of Church life." In addition to the synods the annual assemblies where the clergy formed a compact group also provided a forum for the discussion of ecclesiastical discipline and organization. The mingling of secular and religious matters in the king's meetings with his magnates is reflected in the royal capitularies in which they are intricately combined—for example, in the capitularies for the *missi*. (*See Reading No. 12.*) The idea of conformity with Roman usage that was applied to Church discipline and organization also extended to the Church liturgy. Under the influence of the Anglo-Saxon Alcuin, Charles turned to Pope Hadrian and introduced the *Sacramentarium Gregorianum* sent to him by the pope as the unified liturgy for the Frankish Church. (*See Reading No. 17D.*)

Of course, as head of the Frankish Church, Charles had his own bishops, who served him in any capacity he desired. It is true that they were formally chosen for their office by the local clergy, but no real initiative was left to them. Charles had only to indicate his choice and his nominee would be elected. Since he was sincerely religious and deeply interested in the morals of his people, lay and cleric alike, his choices were usually good ones. The pope would seldom have had any objections to them on moral grounds. Charles was especially careful to keep strict control over the religious work with the newly converted Saxons; he was determined to give them as good an administration as possible and, above all, to destroy pagan religion and customs among them. (*See Reading No. 6.*)

Charles as Theologian: Iconoclasm. But in the realm of faith in which Charles might have been expected to submit to the judgment of the pope, his religious superior, he in fact submitted to no one. He listened to the advice of his Frankish clerics, especially to Alcuin, and then pronounced his own opinion. There is clear evidence that the pope was shocked and dismayed by some of the theological positions taken by Charles; but he had to bow to them.

When Irene became regent in Constantinople for her son Constantine VI, whom she later supplanted, she caused an ecumenical council to be called for the purpose of reconsidering the Church position on the veneration of images. To this council Pope Hadrian sent two representatives; but the Carolingian clergy were not invited, nor did any representatives attend. This Second Council of Nicaea, held in 787, proceeded to lay down the principle that images were worthy of honor, though not to be adored, since adoration is reserved to God. Since this was an improvement on the iconoclasm of Irene's predecessors, the papal legates made no objection. But Charles and his advisers were furious. They received a badly translated account of the Council, which, without the Franks, could hardly be considered ecumenical (universal). (*See Reading No. 15*A.) From this account it appeared that Constantinople and the papacy had reverted to image worship, which in its extreme form was detestable not only to Charles but probably to the majority of his people. Charles sent the report of the Council to Alcuin and others of his theologians, who between them composed a reply known as the *libri Carolini*. This work characterized the Council as a "most inept synod," not a true ecumenical council, and called for the abolition of the worship and adoration of images, stating that "images have hardly any function in the performance of the mystery that involves our salvation." (*See Reading No. 15*B.) God alone, the theologians declared, should be worshipped and adored. This position, incidentally, was not far removed from that of the very council of Nicaea which was being so severely criticized.

Not content with publishing the *libri Carolini* Charles

addressed a long capitulary to Pope Hadrian condemn-
ing image worship a few years later in even more severe terms. (*See Reading No. 15c.*) The pope at first
reacted strongly against this dictation from the Frankish
king, but finally resigned himself to the position taken
by Charles and the Frankish clergy. There can be no
doubt, however, that the submission of the pope to his
protector in a theological matter redounded greatly to
the prestige of the monarch, whose right to dictate had
been so signally demonstrated.

The Adoptionist Heresy. Charles also took decisive
action himself when his kingdom was threatened by the
revival of an old heresy (Nestorianism) in a new version.
This heresy, known as adoptionism, arose in Spain, promulgated by no less a personage than Eliphand, archbishop of Toledo and primate of Spain, a Christian prelate in a land ruled by Muslims and thus personally safe
from the sanctions of pope or Frankish monarch. Eliphand
claimed that the three persons of the Trinity were un-
equal, the Son being inferior to the other two Persons,
since he was not born the Son of God but became the Son
of God only through adoption and grace. This heresy,
when it was drawn to the attention of Pope Hadrian, received a severe condemnation in a letter sent to the Spanish bishops, but it received wider currency when it was
taken up by the learned and pious Bishop Felix of Urgel
in the Spanish March. The latter was made to recant at
a synod called by Charlemagne at the instance of the
pope. Returning to Spain shortly afterward, he relapsed
into his heresy and published his reasons at considerable
length.

Charles then called another synod (794) at Frankfort
and presided over it, taking a leading part in the discussion.
(*See Reading No. 15d.*) The synod proceeded to discuss
not only this new heresy of adoptionism, on the basis of
reports received from Spain, but also the iconoclastic
question. Hadrian, who did not approve of the views of
the Frankish clergy on icons, refused to recognize the
proceedings of this synod as valid. Meanwhile, the adoptionist heresy continued. Pope Leo III condemned the
treatises of Felix as heretical, as did some of the Frankish
clergy, who were at one with the pope on this question.

Charles again summoned the erring bishop to Frankland, and this time Felix was so anxious to present his views publicly that he left the protection of the Spanish archbishop and appeared in person. After a spirited public debate Felix acknowledged himself vanquished, and was sentenced to honorable confinement in Lyons. Interest in the heresy appears to have died down in Spain, although Eliphand maintained it to his death against the opinions of the greater number of his theologians.

The Filioque Controversy. In a third theological controversy Charles intervened decisively. This controversy concerned the procession of the Holy Spirit, on which the Churches in East and West differed, and differ to this day. The Roman Catholic Church includes in its creed the statement that the Holy Spirit is descended from the Father *and* the Son (*filioque*); eastern theologians took the position that the Holy Spirit is descended from the Father *through* the Son. It might be thought that there is no great difference between the two positions. But on closer examination the difference is seen to be fundamental. According to the Orthodox Church there is a "procession" of the three Persons of the Trinity. God the Father begot the Son, through whose death and resurrection the Holy Spirit came to man, and now works in him. In the Roman teaching the Holy Spirit is sent by both the other two Persons of the Trinity, and is at one with them. The whole Trinity therefore works in man, and not the Holy Spirit alone, as in the doctrine of the Orthodox Church. Thus, as a matter of historical fact, the Roman teaching has meant the blurring of the distinction between the third member of the Trinity and the other two. The difference between the two positions is therefore far from a trivial one.

It had been customary in the Western churches to take for granted the procession of the Holy Spirit from both the Father and the Son, following the great African Father of the Church, St. Augustine, and Pope Gregory I, though some Greek Fathers had taken the alternative view. At the second ecumenical council of Nicaea, already referred to, the patriarch of Constantinople had used the formula "through the Son" (*per filium*), and the papal legates had made no protest. It seemed likely that they felt that any altercation on the subject would have driven a further wedge between the two Churches, which had for so many years been at odds over the iconoclastic controversy. The Frankish theologians, however, had protested in the *libri Carolini*. In turn Pope Hadrian rebuked the Franks for their interference and defended the *per filium* as being a legitimate point of view to hold, supported by the authority of some of the Church Fathers. Alcuin in a work on the Trinity published in 802 came out strongly for the position of the Frankish Church.

But the problem was far from settled. The Greeks took the initiative in 808 and treated some Latin monks in Palestine as heretics for adding the word *filioque* to the Mass. The monks appealed both to Pope Leo III and to Charlemagne, who was now emperor, saying that they had heard the formula in use at Aachen in the royal chapel. Charles, now that his attention had again been drawn to the controversy, had Theodulfus, one of his leading theologians, draw up another statement, defending the *filioque*. He then summoned a council which met at Aachen and pronounced in its favor. Pope Leo refused to accept the competence of the Council in such a matter. He did not object to the formula as a matter of doctrine, but refused to insert it into the Mass, no doubt because of his anxiety not to offend the Byzantines and exacerbate the differences between the two Churches. Not indeed, until two centuries had passed did a later pope permit it, though the patriarch of Constantinople as early as 867 attacked the western Church for holding the doctrine of the *filioque*. Ultimately, in the middle of the eleventh century, when the Orthodox Church was definitively severed from the Roman, this same theological question bulked large among the differences between the two Churches.

Summary: Charles as Caesaropapist. These instances of the interference of Charles and his theologians in matters of dogma demonstrate clearly enough the emperor's belief that he was as much head of the Church as head of the State. Far back in time at the end of the fifth century Pope Gelasius I had propounded the doctrine of the Two Authorities. (*See Reading No. 16A.*) According to this doctrine, authority on earth belongs to both Church and State, whose fields of jurisdiction are separate. The civil magistrate is in charge of the maintenance of peace, order, and justice, while spiritual interests and salvation are in the keeping of the Church. The clergy is in charge of all doctrinal matters and is independent and self-governing. It should have full jurisdiction over ecclesiastics. According to Gelasius, clerics should even be tried for all offenses by ecclesiastical courts. No man should be both priest and king, but each has need of the other. The king needs the priest for the sake of his salvation, and the priest needs an orderly society to enable him to exercise his proper care of souls. Even so, the priest has a higher responsibility than the monarch, for the Church is concerned with eternal salvation, which the monarch himself can attain only with its aid. But under the Gelasian doctrine, which remained authoritative throughout the Middle Ages, when it was propounded more picturesquely as the doctrine of the Two Swords (*see Readings Nos. 16*c *and 16*D), it was not believed that this separation of the roles of Church and State should lead to conflict between the two. It was believed possible that each could attend to its own duties without infringing on those of the other.

It is clear that such a doctrine was not that held by Charlemagne, nor did any pope in his day dare to suggest it to him. Charles in his own view was responsible for both Church and State. He had no inhibitions about issuing ordinances for the clergy, reminding them of their moral duties; nor did he hesitate to make full use of the services of clerics when he needed them. He disciplined them also when he felt it to be necessary. When Leo III became pope, Charlemagne sent a letter even to him, instructing him to set a good example to Christians in his own behavior and setting forth his views on their respective roles. (*See Reading No. 16*B.) There is no known case where Charles ever deferred to the opinion of either pope or cleric by virtue of the fact that they were clergymen and held the keys to salvation. He often consulted his own clerics, especially Alcuin. But the advice had to be acceptable to him or he would not follow it. He regarded even such a man as Alcuin as wholly within his jurisdiction and under his orders. He required him to attend his court or his General Assembly, and refused to accept any excuse for nonattendance save infirmity.

When there was famine or disaster in the land it was Charles who commanded the special prayers and fasts; when he had won a great military victory, it was he who decreed the thanksgivings. He issued ordinances dealing with such religious matters as baptism and the sacraments, and took steps to see that his clergy obeyed them. He made arrangements for the education of the clergy, and he instructed bishops in their pastoral duties. He reminded his monks to obey strictly the rule of St. Benedict. (*See Reading No. 12.*)

But the peculiar feature of all this activity is that at least the Frankish clergy appear not to have resented it. On the contrary, they seem to have welcomed it, and constantly praised the pious zeal of the emperor. Time after time the records show them asking for the benefit of his opinion, and they submitted even dogmatic propositions for his judgment. Popes Hadrian and Leo, it is true, on occasion felt, as we have seen, that Charles was usurping their functions when he pronounced on matters of dogma. It is possible, indeed, to read some irritation beneath the polite phrases of some of the letters of Hadrian. Charles, on the other hand, evidently regarded the popes as faithful collaborators in his work, and he took it for granted that they could not but approve of his efforts to reform the clergy and lift them out of the degradation of the Merovingian age. He was so sure of his right to dictate to the clergy and supervise their morals and behavior as well as their administration, that probably no one in his day thought of questioning him, not even the pope. Looking back at the reign of Charlemagne from the vantage point of the twentieth century, we can only marvel at the ease with which this illiterate ruler was able to concern himself with so much and exercise in so many fields his completely unquestioned supremacy without exciting so much as a breath of opposition, save for a small handful of rebellious nobles. Never again was any western ruler to be able to dictate to the Church, and few were able to command such obedience from their subjects.

Charlemagne's chosen reading was St. Augustine's *City of God.* "Happy is the ruler," St. Augustine had said, "who uses his power to propagate the worship of God . . . who allows himself to be led not by the desire for

useless glory, but by the love of eternal happiness." Charles
on his deathbed without doubt believed that this had been
his aim and he had fulfilled it worthily. If he was a caesaropapist, it had been in the interests of his Christian
people; he had not humiliated the pope, nor had he subjected him to his will. He had merely made use of him
for his own higher aims, which were necessarily shared
by the head of the Church. He had not been a tyrant and
he had not been arbitrary. He had ruled with justice and
equity. He had lived up to the vows of his coronation. Regarding himself as responsible only to God for his empire,
it cannot be denied that he tried as fully as he could to
live up to the responsibility. It is difficult to point to another ruler in Christendom of whom so much can be said;
and certainly there has been no other whose power was as
great as his and who misused it so little—"a chief in
whose shadow," as Alcuin put it, "the people of Christendom rest in peace, and who inspires terror among heathen
nations."

— 5 —

THE CAROLINGIAN RENAISSANCE

Contrast with Other "Renaissances." Sixty years ago
almost all Europeans knew of only one "renaissance," that
of the fourteenth, fifteenth, and sixteenth centuries, which
saw the rebirth of Western culture after the "long dark
night" of the Middle Ages. It was thought that Western
man suddenly awoke and after long neglect of his heritage
from Greece and Rome became once more aware of the
world around him. He acquired a new interest in life on
earth and ceased to be exclusively preoccupied with salvation after death. The works of the nineteenth-century
writers Burckhardt and Symonds were so appealing and

convincing that they laid their impress on several generations of historians, whose views in turn percolated down
to the public in general. Thus even today for most people
the Renaissance means the revival of the classics and the
great outpouring of artistic masterpieces characteristic of
fifteenth- and sixteenth-century Italy.

Today, when our knowledge of the Middle Ages is
much wider than it was at the turn of the century, two
tendencies have become visible. On the one hand, many
historians, especially medievalists, have tended to stress
the continuity of culture between the Middle Ages and
the early modern period, and have played down the notion of a true Renaissance at any time in the history of
Western man. The works of each epoch, for these historians, are dependent on the achievements of the previ-
ous one, and are unthinkable without them. On the other
hand, there has also been a tendency to look for other
renaissances, in some respects the equal of the most famous one.

Among such renaissances may be noted the Carolingian
Renaissance, which consisted primarily of the revival of
interest in the Latin classics, and the recovery of skill in
Latin composition, coupled with a strong impetus toward
the improvement and expansion of education. This "renaissance" was, however, but a flash in the pan, since the
renewed barbarian invasions (Norsemen and Magyars)
and the political difficulties attending the breakup of the
Carolingian empire created conditions in most of Europe
unfavorable to the spread of learning. German historians
like to speak of an "Ottonian renaissance" in the late tenth
century under the inspiration of Otto the Great, refounder
of the empire. Charles Homer Haskins wrote a famous
book in 1927 (*The Renaissance of the Twelfth Century*),
which drew attention to the extensive revival of the study
of Latin classics, of the creation of Latin literature on
their model, and of Roman Law and the beginning of the
flow of translations of Aristotle from the Arabic, following the reconquest of Spain by the Christians, as well as
a renewed interest in translating direct from the Greek.
This twelfth-century renaissance prepared the way for the
full flowering of medieval culture in the thirteenth century. The work of none of these renaissances was totally

lost; none would have achieved what they did without having the work of their predecessors to build upon.

There can be no doubt that interest in intellectual inquiry reached a low ebb in the Merovingian kingdom. The few literate men of the period were to be found in the ranks of the clergy; but even so the bulk of the clergy was absorbed in secular interests, and totally uneducated. Only in a few of the monasteries was there a feeble glimmer of learning, and even that bore no comparison at all with the knowledge widely available in the same epoch in Ireland and England.

The Carolingian Renaissance essentially consisted in the transfer from Ireland and England, Italy and Spain, to the land of the Franks of the tools for learning. These tools were then put to use in Carolingian territories by the authority and under the inspiration of the Carolingian monarchs. It was, therefore, primarily an educational reform, which gave birth to a new class of literate men and women who then in their turn produced works in a relatively pure Latin idiom. Charles himself was interested also in the vernacular language and literature, especially in the old lays written in the Germanic tongue, although his efforts to stimulate interest in these does not appear to have been highly successful. But the educational impulse instituted by him was able to survive in attenuated form even in the chaotic political conditions accompanying the breakup of the empire.

Alcuin and the Palace School. The unquestioned leader of the educational movement was Alcuin, an English deacon who had been educated in York and who came to the attention of Charles when he was returning from a mission to Rome. He was then already about fifty years of age. Charles offered him the headship of the palace school at Aachen, which he planned to develop as the center of his educational venture. After consulting his king and archbishop, Alcuin decided to accept the responsibility. He worked at Aachen for fifteen years, and was then prevailed upon by Charles to continue in his kingdom, as abbot of St. Martin of Tours, where he remained until his death in 804. Although not an original writer nor a man of exceptional intellectual attainment, he was beloved as a teacher, and his advice was constantly sought, both by

Charles and the scholars and teachers who were brought together by the monarch. He had also a very clear idea of the political role of his master, especially in his relations with the papacy. Throughout the extant letters of Alcuin there is always visible his constant concern with political problems. As L. Wallach has recently shown, Alcuin's influence on Charles's political ideas, especially on his imperial role, can hardly be overestimated. Alcuin was also able to provide the theological foundations for Charles's actions with regard to iconoclasm, the adoptionist heresy, and the trinitarian controversy with Constantinople. Wallach found that Alcuin was the editor of the *libri Carolini*.

The palace school at Aachen, though far from a university of the medieval type, remained the leading educational institution of the reign of Charles and performed some of the functions of a university. It was in existence already before the reign of Charlemagne, but in earlier reigns it appears to have fulfilled the task of training royal princes and the sons of leading nobles. It had never stressed intellectual training; it attempted rather to inculcate those martial virtues approved of by the warrior aristocracy and monarchs. Under Alcuin it ceased to be a school merely for youths, nor was it restricted to the higher nobility. It opened its doors to young men of promise from all classes who had been brought to the attention of Charles or Alcuin. Many of the great teachers and writers of the generation following Charles received their education there and went out into the world afterward to take up important positions in the imperial services, either as clerics or laymen. Elementary education under severe discipline was given, as well as more advanced education for more mature students. The latter teaching appears to have been quite informal. It was marked by an easy camaraderie and a fellowship both between teachers and taught and between the students themselves.

The students and teachers gave one another nicknames derived from classical antiquity or the Bible. After they had left the palace school to take up their positions in the world, they continued to correspond with one another and with their old teachers. All this suggests that these few privileged persons, a tiny group of literate and educated men in an almost wholly illiterate world, were very conscious of the difference between them and their contemporaries, and that their period at the palace school was looked back to with sentimental affection at a time when, for once in their lives, they had lived among others with whom they could converse on intimate terms as equals—a condition which would never recur once they were out in the world on their own in responsible positions among men who had never known Alcuin and his fellow scholars.

It is certain that for a number of years Charles had a deep interest in his school at a period when his empire was prospering and conditions were relatively stable, before the great revolt of the recently conquered Saxons. Though he never lost interest in it, never afterwards could he devote so much of his time to it as during those few years. He paid visits to the school whenever he could, and when the other responsibilities of his life permitted it. He is pictured in episodic stories by the monk of St. Gall as discussing the educational content of the school with Alcuin, encouraging and reproving, and even, on occasion, personally disciplining the students, invariably showing his enlightened concern with what was being done under his patronage and in his name at the school.

Cathedral and Monastery Schools. The palace school was the center of the educational reform of Charlemagne, since it provided a nucleus of teachers who could be given responsibilities in all parts of the kingdom. But the outstanding work of the reign was the establishment of the medieval educational system itself. Charles issued whole capitularies dealing with education and learning. He expected every diocese and monastery to have its own school. His main concern was with literacy, since, as he said, he had recognized in most of the letters he had received "both correct thoughts and uncouth expressions," and he began to fear that the meaning of the gospels would be lost through corruption of the texts. (*See Reading No. 17*A.) It was for the purpose of improving grammar and syntax above all that he urged the heads of monasteries and cathedrals to establish schools of liberal arts.

Charlemagne sent for the most distinguished scholars and educators he could find in his domains or outside them, and made them bishops and abbots. For example,

Theodulf was brought from Spain and made bishop of Orléans, where he set to work with vigor. He organized four major schools in his diocese, which were not reserved for those destined for the priesthood, but were open to all who wished to enter. He called upon his country priests to organize free schools for pupils from the seigneurial and free villages, where at least the rudiments of education would be taught. He also instructed his pastors to give regular Sunday sermons to his parishioners. Other bishops followed the same practice. Bishop Leidrad of Lyons reported that he had endeavored to carry out the ordinances of the emperor in establishing schools in his diocese. A council held at Mainz in 813 recommended that children should be sent to school, either to monasteries or to schools run by priests, so that each catechumen should, if nothing else, be instructed in the basic teachings of the Christian faith.

The new schools of Charlemagne had also to provide education for readers, singers, assistants, copyists, and writers, as well as for potential clergymen, as had the few schools that existed before his time. (*See Readings Nos. 17B to 17D.*) But there was one startling innovation which caused some dismay, especially among the upper classes. Charles wished the children of both freemen and nobles to go to these schools. But he succeeded better in persuading the children from the lower classes to go, since the nobles were as anxious as in later times to avoid too intimate contact with their social inferiors. The preponderance of children from the lower classes in the schools meant that the newly educated clergy, among whom there were many who had previously been serfs, filled at least the lower ranks of the hierarchy. But it was not impossible for low-born men to achieve high positions in the Church that had been customarily reserved for the aristocracy, where, as might be imagined, many of them assumed the manners of their betters, to the frequent disgust of the old nobility.

In the monasteries, on the other hand, the majority of pupils were destined to become monks, and not ordained clergymen. It was from the monasteries that most of the theologians were drawn. The busy bishop had so many administrative tasks to perform in his diocese, as well as for his monarch, that he could not hope to become as learned as a monk or an abbot. But the monasteries also set up schools for the education of all those children in the neighborhood who wished to receive some education. In these schools the discipline was very strict, but many of them obtained an enviable reputation for the learning they imparted. Thus literacy and the rudiments of learning became gradually far better distributed than in the past, and a nucleus of educated men became available for the numerous tasks both in the Church and in government where literacy was a prerequisite.

Curriculum of the Schools. The curriculum of the palace school and other schools in the Carolingian age was founded upon the so-called liberal arts. The notion that all education could be fitted into the mold of seven liberal arts stems from a somewhat fantastic treatise by Martianus Capella, a Roman of the Late Empire, entitled *The Nuptials of Mercury and Philology*. This book, which dressed up its educational material in a mythological and allegorical story, greatly appealed to the medieval mind, persuading generations of educators that there must be seven such "arts" and only seven. The Carolingian educators may have been the first to divide these seven arts into two groups, although the feat has been ascribed to many others, including the sixth-century Roman Boethius, whose textbooks on various arts became so popular in the Middle Ages. These arts were the *trivium*—grammar, rhetoric, and dialectic; and the *quadrivium*—arithmetic, music, geometry, and astronomy. It became customary to regard the trivium as the more basic general education, and the quadrivium as more advanced. Together with theology the liberal arts encompassed the whole range of the interests and were responsible for the intellectual ferment of the scholars gathered or trained at the palace school. (*See Reading No. 17*E.)

There was little or no interest in scientific speculation, and almost no knowledge of Greek. With regard to Latin the situation was somewhat different. There was a long tradition, of which Pope Gregory I (590-604) and Gregory of Tours were exponents, that the non-Christian works of classical antiquity were likely to lead men away from the Christian path. In the Carolingian age this tradition was represented by two influential writers. But the more common viewpoint was that the works of Latin literature should be used for practical purposes, namely, to obtain a thorough knowledge of the Latin language. The study of Latin grammar by itself did not suffice, for it could not be studied in a vacuum. The student had also to understand how the rules of grammar and style had been used by the great classical writers. In general, the scholars of the Carolingian period were not, in fact, so much interested in the contents of the books they read as in the book itself—unless the book happened to be concerned with a subject that was of practical use to them. They loved to own and read books, whether profane or religious; and it is to this urge that we owe the preservation of so many manuscripts of classical antiquity, which were preserved for posterity only by the diligence of Carolingian scholars and copyists.

The manuscripts of many important Latin works available today stem from Carolingian copies. The result of the intensive study of Latin language and literature was the partial restoration of the correct Latin language, as it had been used in the classical period, and a considerable improvement in Latin style, observable in the best writings of the Carolingian age. Incidentally, this was also one of the achievements of the later Italian Renaissance, though more difficult to achieve in the later period when medieval Latin had evolved much further than it had in the eighth and ninth centuries.

Under the heading of "grammar" both the rudiments of the Latin language and Latin literature were included. The elementary grammar was based on the *Ars minor,* the fourth-century grammatical treatise of Donatus, teacher of St. Jerome, the distinguished translator of the Vulgate and one of the Latin Fathers of the Church. A more advanced treatise of Donatus, the *Ars major,* together with a work by the sixth-century Latin writer Priscian, were evidently in use in some educational centers, but not in wide general use. Clemens Scotus, a teacher in Charlemagne's palace school, compiled a grammar of his own, making use of the writings of many classical authors, as well as the grammatical works of his predecessors. Many new grammatical works appeared in the ninth century, as, for example, Alcuin's *Ars grammatica,* often written for the benefit of the writers' own pupils. The teachers tried to convey to their pupils the concrete meaning of words they used, and much of their instruction took the form of dialogues between teachers and pupils. (*See Readings Nos. 17*F *and 17*G.)

With regard to the other two subjects of the *trivium,* Cicero's works on rhetoric and some others were widely used. But two textbooks compiled by Alcuin on logic and rhetoric, neither of them at all advanced, were probably the main sources of information. The study of mathematics was hindered by the absence of an effective arithmetical notation, while Euclid, for geometry, was not available to the Carolingians. All they possessed were some simplified textbooks by Boethius and Bede. Astronomy was used primarily for the computation of the church calendar. Boethius and Isidore of Seville were the older authorities. But more recent works by the Englishman, the Venerable Bede, were available in all libraries. Charles himself was very much interested in astronomy, and frequently corresponded with Alcuin about the stars after the latter had left the court. (*See Reading No. 17*E.) Theoretical music was studied also from a text by Boethius, and much care was given to the singing of hymns and the liturgy. In the singing and other details of the church service Charles showed a personal interest. (*See Reading No. 17*D.)

Libraries and Scriptoria. In the time of Charlemagne all the cathedral schools and monasteries had their libraries, however ill stocked some of them might be. In the days before printing the only way to increase the holding of a library was either to borrow a manuscript from another library, copy it, and return it, keeping the copy; or to purchase a copy from a *scriptorium* or writing school which specialized in the production of such copies and had a few available for sale. Though a number of cathedral schools had their own *scriptoria*—for example, Lyons, Metz, Würzburg, Reims, and Cologne—most of the *scriptoria* were to be found at the monasteries— perhaps because the abbot had more time available than a busy bishop and had at his disposal more men who could be trained to become copyists than were available to most bishops. The collections of books at Reichenau, Corbie, Fulda, St. Gall, and other great monasteries were very considerable and included sometimes excellent libraries of classical works. The *scriptorium* at Reichenau bustled with activity, and manuscripts were often given as gifts as well as sold. Five booklists from the period 821-846 survive; the earliest list contains more than 400 writers. Murbach in the Vosges around 850 possessed rare authors like Lucretius and Frontinus. Few could vie with Bobbio, however, the monastery in north central Italy that had been founded in 612 by St. Columban. Here there were between six and seven hundred titles, with a great array of sacred and profane authors. Fulda had codices of Tacitus, the Letters of Pliny, the agricultural work of Columella, and others. When Alcuin became abbot of St. Martin de Tours after retiring from the palace school at Aachen, he naturally devoted much of his attention to stocking the monastery library, using his English connections to obtain rare manuscripts from York and elsewhere.

It was in some eighth-century monastery—there is still dispute among scholars as to which was the pioneer—that the script known as Carolingian minuscule was devised. The oldest extant example of a manuscript in this writing is a multivolumed Bible written in Corbie about 778. Carolingian minuscule was a clear beautiful script that is the direct ancestor of our own. Gradually through the period of a century it replaced the difficult but beautiful uncial and half-uncial scripts, and the almost unreadable Merovingian cursive that was a corruption of the Roman cursive.

Carolingian Literature—Latin. The literary achievements of the reigns of Charlemagne and, more particularly, of his Carolingian successors were not inconsiderable—and very considerable indeed if they are compared with those of the Merovingian era. Ninth-century achievements are, of course, directly due to the educational impulse of the reign of Charles and to the encouragement given to all forms of literary activity by the monarch himself. The great men of his reign—Alcuin, Paul the Deacon, Theodulf—were all poets in the Latin language as well as theologians, historians, and often administrators. The men corresponded with one another in verse and often addressed the emperor himself in verse couplets. Theodulf in a poem has described for posterity the personalities and individual traits of the court circle: the great monarch presiding over a banquet; Alcuin, also a hearty eater, surrounded by young men, offering good moral advice and being listened to with respect fitting his years; Einhard, the biographer of Charlemagne, small and bustling, "a small body which houses a great spirit." (*See Reading No. 17H.*) The whole picture suggests court circles of other ages and realms.

The circle was small, and Charles himself was rarely free enough of his other immense responsibilities to take an active share in it. But it was virtually his own creation; it was only his continued patronage that made it possible. For a period a number of distinguished foreigners stayed in Frankland at his invitation, either at the palace school or elsewhere. Peter of Pisa, a grammarian, and Paul the Deacon, a historian and grammarian, were among these guests. The latter taught in Metz, where he composed a history of the bishops of his diocese. When he returned to Italy he wrote the very popular *History of the Lombards,* almost our only source for the early history of this people. Einhard wrote an outstanding biography of Charlemagne, which is perhaps the best literary production in prose that emanated from the palace school.

Vernacular Literature. In his biography of Charlemagne, Einhard tells us that his master was deeply interested in the older Germanic poems, which he caused to be written down. He began, as Einhard says, a "grammar of his native tongue." (*See Reading No. 18A.*) He gave German names to the months and to the winds, names which are unknown elsewhere and evidently did not survive. Unfortunately almost none of this vernacular literature, which must have been composed mainly of epic poems, has come down to us. A fragment of the *Lay of Hildebrand* exists in one version, which may belong to the age of Charlemagne. The text was written in Fulda on the back of a Latin manuscript. The Gospel Book of Otfrid of Weissenburg, written in Old High German verse, however, was certainly an outcome of Charles's interest in the vernacular tongue. (*See Reading No. 18D.*) The author was a monk trained at the monastery of Fulda, a disciple of Hrabanus Maurus, who had studied at Tours with Alcuin. The purpose of this poem was to reveal the truths of the Gospel to those who would never learn Latin. Another long religious poem in the vernacular was the *Heliand* (Savior) by an unknown writer in the time of Louis the Pious, successor of Charlemagne. This poem was written in Old Low German (Saxon) using old Anglo-Saxon metres. In this poem Jesus Christ is depicted as a kind of Teutonic ruler and his disciples as noble lords owing fidelity and allegiance to him.

Perhaps the most important result of the royal encouragement of the vernacular languages was its effect on religious instruction. The Saxon converts were instructed in the truths of their new religion in the German language (*see Reading No. 18*B), and Charles commanded that the priests should have their sermons translated into either the Romance or German tongues for the benefit of those who understood no Latin. (*See Reading No. 18*C.) Although these translations are no longer extant, they were certainly made, and interlinear glosses, vocabularies, and other aids to the study of the Scriptures are known from this period and the succeeding reigns. Though Charles did more for the German language than for the Romance languages, the oldest existing document in any of the Romance languages was drawn up in the time of his grandsons. The famous Oaths of Strasburg, by which two grandsons of Charlemagne agreed in 842 not to enter into a separate peace with the third brother Lothair, with whom they were at war, were drawn up in German and Romance. (*See Reading No. 18*E.) The fact that it was possible to make such an oath in the language then used in France may well also have been a result of Charles's encouragement of the vernacular, and of the fact that, under his inspiration, the language popularly spoken in the western parts of Frankland was first written down as well as spoken.

The most important result of the efforts of Charles and his collaborators was the increase of literacy in his territories. If it was too early to expect much scholarship, and especially not original scholarship, the foundations for the future were, nevertheless, truly laid. The ninth century could boast of a number of superior scholars and a few truly original works. The most remarkable original philosophical work to appear in several centuries was the *De divisione naturae* of John Scotus Erigena, who worked at the court of Charles the Bald, grandson of Charlemagne. John would never have found a patron in Charles the Bald if it had not been for the work of Charlemagne, nor might he ever have gone to France from his native Ireland if the literary climate had not been transformed in that country by the great emperor.

Carolingian Art. The Carolingian age was not one of the great ages of art, but there were several innovations in Charles's reign which were to have considerable importance in the future. The innovations in themselves were not original, but they were new in Frankish lands and were largely the result of Charles's conquests in Italy and a desire to compete in some small degree with the great imperial capital on the Bosporus. Charles, in particular, wished to beautify Aachen, his own capital, and make it more worthy of his imperial position. (*See Reading No. 19A.*) He built a round church in honor of the Virgin Mary on the model of the Byzantine church of San Vitale at Ravenna, built by Justinian; and he purloined classical columns from Ravenna to add to it. These columns were replaced in later structures by stone piers, since classical columns were no longer available for transfer once the imperial period was over. The cupola was decorated with golden mosaics representing scenes from the Apocalypse—the first time such mosaics had been used in any Germanic church, though they were to become a prominent feature of later Romanesque churches. This "palace chapel" of Aachen was to provide a model for many other Carolingian churches. But the round church was not really suited for the developing Christian ritual in the West and was soon to be replaced by the true early Romanesque. The palaces planned by Charlemagne, most of which were not carried to completion and which, being built of wood, did not survive the Norse invasions, had little of architectural interest, as far as is known, though Ravenna was sometimes again used as a model.

The Mediterranean influence on the minor arts was both more profound and more lasting. The older Germanic art had been largely confined to the decoration of weapons and ordinary utensils, such as drinking horns, and for personal ornamentation. This ornamentation, unlike Greek, Roman, and Byzantine work, was abstract and often fantastic rather than representational. The Christians in the Byzantine empire and in Italy had, however, developed representational art—art which, making use of human figures, could tell a story and thus serve for religious propaganda and education. No doubt Charles was interested in the heritage of the Roman Empire, which he believed himself to have inherited; but it was of more importance to him to make use of art for practical religious purposes. (*See Reading No. 19B.*)

The illustration and illumination of manuscripts with lively and dramatic pictures, an art which was carried to such a wonderful degree of refinement in the later Middle Ages, really may be said to date from the reign of Charlemagne. Before his grandsons were in the grave, many of the illuminations of Westerners had already far surpassed the work of their original teachers. Some Bibles had been illustrated before the time of Charlemagne, but always with abstract decorations. The taste for these and for geometrical forms was not lost, and some of the Carolingian and post-Carolingian books continue to betray the interest of the artists in their abstractions rather than in the human forms. In this respect, therefore, it may be said that Carolingian art is a synthesis of Germanic and Mediterranean elements as well as something genuinely new.

Many of the monasteries as well as the imperial palace had workshops attached to them where books were decorated and where ivory was carved into diptychs showing religious scenes. These arts were never lost, even in the troubled conditions attending the breakup of the Carolingian empire, for the models were to be seen and imitated wherever Carolingian influence had spread.

Summary and Conclusion. It will be clear from the foregoing rather meager list of the accomplishments of the "Carolingian renaissance" that its total achievement was slight, especially if one compares it with the other ages that have been granted the title of "renaissance." But if it is viewed from a different angle and is not judged on the basis of either quantity or quality, but rather on the basis of what it transmitted to future generations, the balance sheet will appear more favorable. The copying of so many manuscripts, even from the classical age of Rome, certainly preserved many works of literature, of which we should otherwise have been deprived. The Carolingian renaissance did revive and enlarge education in both cathedral and monastery schools, and a fair number of scholars obtained a respectable knowledge of the Latin language and literature. The men whose education had been sponsored by Charlemagne and their successors kept alight the torch of learning in the ages of anarchy that followed.

The renaissance did not die with the great monarch whose name it bore. Charles the Bald, the grandson of Charles, enjoyed a far from glorious reign and died miserably; but his court supported John Scotus Erigena and many another writer of less originality. Never after the reign of Charlemagne was there an intellectual regression comparable to that of the Merovingian age. Learning and education survived until the political tide turned and conditions became more favorable for continued growth. If the Carolingian renaissance was but a feeble light shining in an almost Stygian gloom, it was at least a light; that the light in the West was not again extinguished may be in large measure attributed to the mighty impetus given to it by the monarch who assembled the few scholars of his age in his court, favored them with his patronage and encouraged them by his enthusiasm.

Part II—READINGS

— Reading No. 1 —

MEROVINGIAN MONARCHY AND ARISTOCRACY

The readings of the first series illustrate the new order in Frankish Gaul under the early Merovingians. Reading 1A tells of the new absolute power of the monarch over the tribal freemen who had formerly possessed customary rights on which no king could trample; 1B shows the resentment of the Frankish freemen at being compelled to pay tolls and taxes into the royal coffers; 1C is an extract from a precept of Clothar II recognizing the legal limits of the royal power; 1D is taken from the Edict of Clothar of 614, in which the monarch consents to certain limitations of his powers.

✓   ✓   ✓

A. *From Gregory of Tours,* History of the Franks[1]

II, 27 . . . At that time many churches were despoiled by Clovis' army, since he was as yet involved in heathen error. Now the army had taken from a certain church a vase of wonderful size and beauty, along with the remainder of the utensils for the service of the church. And the bishop of the church sent messengers to the king asking that the vase at least be returned, if he could not get back any more of the sacred dishes. On hearing this the king said to the messenger: "Follow us as far as Soissons, because all that has been taken is to be divided there and

[1] From Gregory, Bishop of Tours, *History of the Franks.* Selections translated with notes by Ernest Bréhaut (New York, 1916), pp. 37-38.

when the lot assigns me that dish I will do what the father[1] asks." Then when he came to Soissons and all the booty was set in their midst, the king said: "I ask of you, brave warriors, not to refuse to grant me in addition to my share, yonder dish," that is, he was speaking of the vase just mentioned. In answer to the speech of the king those of more sense replied: "Glorious king, all that we see is yours, and we ourselves are subject to your rule. Now do what seems well-pleasing to you; for no one is able to resist your power." When they said this a foolish, envious and excitable fellow lifted his battle-ax and struck the vase, and cried in a loud voice: "You shall get nothing here except what the lot fairly bestows on you." At this all were stupefied, but the king endured the insult with the gentleness of patience, and taking the vase he handed it over to the messenger of the church, nursing the wound deep in his heart. And at the end of the year he ordered the whole army to come with their equipment of armor to show the brightness of their arms on the field of March. And when he was reviewing them all carefully, he came to the man who struck the vase and said to him: "No one has brought armor so carelessly kept as you; for neither your spear nor sword nor ax is in serviceable condition." And seizing his ax he cast it to the earth, and when the other had bent over somewhat to pick it up, the king raised his hands and drove his own ax into the man's head. "This," said he, "is what you did at Soissons to the vase." Upon the death of this man, he ordered the rest to depart raising great dread of himself by this action. . . .

B. *From Gregory of Tours,* History of the Franks[2]

VII, 15 . . . She [Queen Fredegunda] had with her at the time a judge, Audo, who had assisted in many wrongdoings in the time of the king. For together with Mummolus, the prefect, he subjected to the state tax many Franks who in the time of the king Childebert the

---

[1] *papa.* The word was used in the early Middle Ages in unrestricted, informal sense, and applied widely to bishops. *Cf.* Du Cange, *Glossarium.*

[2] Gregory, *loc. cit.,* p. 177.

elder were free born. After the king's death he was despoiled by them and stripped, so that he had nothing left except what he could carry away. For they burned his house and would have taken his life if he had not fled to the church with the queen.

c. From a Precept of Clothar II, 584-628 [1]

3. No one accused of a crime should be condemned without hearing (*inauditus*).

5. If some one has wrested from us a concession (*auctoritas nostra*) against the law (*contra legem*) by deceit this concession will be null and void.

D. From the Edict of Clothar II, 614 [2]

1. It is agreed that . . . after the death of a bishop . . . his successor will be elected by the clergy and the people (*a clero et populo*); if the person is worthy of the office let him be ordained by the king's order; if he is chosen from among the men of the court let it be on account of his personal merits and knowledge (*doctrina*).

8. Wherever a new *census* [land tax] has been introduced and the people complain about it, let it be canceled mercifully after inquiry has been made.

9. Only such tolls should be levied and on such type of merchandise as have been levied by our predecessors. . . .

12. No judge [count] shall be appointed from provinces or regions other than his own. . . .[3]

---

[1] Translated by H.W. from *Capitularia regum Francorum* I (*Monumenta Germaniae Historica, Legum Sectio* II, 1), no. 8, p. 19.

[2] *Ibid.*, no. 9, pp. 21-22.

[3] That is: other than the one he is to administer.

— Reading No. 2 —

THE NEW FRANKISH SOCIETY

Reading 2A shows how the counts of two warring regions stopped a feud by holding a hearing and determining the composition money to be paid by the aggressor. Reading 2B records an address by Bishop Gregory of Tours to the citizens of his episcopal see urging them to bring a blood feud to an end. The reading shows how the bishops were in a position to use the moral and spiritual authority as well as the material resources of the Church in the attempt to reconcile the parties.

✓   ✓   ✓

A. *Bishop Gregory's Account of a Feud* [1]

Now when [King] Chilperic had died and had found the death he had long been looking for, the men of Orleans united with those of Blois made an attack on the people of Chateaudun and defeated them, taking them off their guard; they burned their houses and crops and whatever they could not carry away conveniently, and they plundered flocks and herds and carried off all that was not fast. Upon their departure the men of Chateaudun with the rest of the men of Chartres pursued them closely and treated them in the same way as they were treated, leaving nothing in their houses or outside their houses or of their houses. And while they were still abusing one another and raging, and the men of Orleans were ready to fight the men of Chartres, the counts intervened and at a hearing before them peace was made, on condition that on the day when court was to be held the side which had flamed out wrongfully against the other should make payment according to justice. And thus the war was ended.

[1] From Gregory, *loc. cit.,* VII, 2, p. 172.

B. *Bishop Gregory's Address to the Citizens of Tours*[1]

"Refrain, O men, from further crimes, lest the evil spread more widely. We have already lost sons of our Church in this strife and now we fear more losses. Keep peace, I pray you! Let him who committed the wrong make composition for the sake of charity that you be children of peace, worthy to earn the kingdom of God by the mercy of the Lord. . . . And behold, if he who is found guilty by chance lack the money for the payment he will be redeemed with the money of the Church that no man's soul perish."

— Reading No. 3 —

DECLINE OF LEARNING (AFTER 500)

One of the two writers of major standing representing literary Gaul in the sixth century was the historian, Gregory, Bishop of Tours. Though he includes himself in the process which he describes as "liberal culture on the wane," it is not altogether true that he was "neither imbued with the art of grammar nor learned in the reading of secular authors." Though his Latin is frequently incorrect, his style is simple ("rustic") not by incapacity but on purpose (see the end of 3A). Many passages reflect his appreciation of and his training in contemporary rhetorical style. Neither is his assertion that he had no knowledge of secular Latin literature borne out by his works. But it is true that on principle he rejects pagan learning and that for himself he has resolved the conflict between the two

[1] Translated by H.W. from *Gregorii episcopi Turonensis Historia Francorum*, VII, 47 (*Mon. Germ. Hist., Scriptores rerum Merowingicarum* I), p. 323.

*schools of thought in favor of the orthodox Christian view
which meant "the unqualified condemnation of pagan
literature." In 3B this age-old conflict is represented by
the familiar dream of St. Jerome.*

✓   ✓   ✓

A. *Gregory of Tours Apologizes for His "Rudeness of
Speech"* [1]

With liberal culture on the wane, or rather perishing,
in the Gallic cities, there were many deeds being done
both good and evil: the heathen were raging fiercely; kings
were growing more cruel; the church, attacked by heretics,
was defended by Catholics; while the Christian faith was
in general devoutly cherished by the faithful or plundered
by traitors—and no grammarian skilled in the dialectic art
could be found to describe these matters either in prose
or verse; and many were lamenting and saying: "Woe
to our day, since the pursuit of letters has perished from
among us and no one can be found among the people
who can set forth the deeds of the present on the written
page." Hearing continually these complaints and others
like them I [have undertaken] to commemorate the past,
in order that it may come to the knowledge of the future;
and although my speech is rude, I have been unable to be
silent as to the struggles between the wicked and the
upright; and I have been especially encouraged because,
to my surprise, it has often been said by men of our days,
that few understand the learned words of the rhetorician
but many the rude language of the common people. I
have decided also that for the reckoning of the years the
first book shall begin with the very beginning of the world,
and I have given its chapters below.

B. *Gregory of Tours Explains His Attitude toward
Pagan Authors* [2]

The priest Hieronymus, best teacher of the church after
the apostle Paul, says that he was led before the judgment

---

[1] Gregory, *History of the Franks, loc. cit.*, p. 1 (from Preface
to Book I).
[2] Gregory of Tours, *Selections from the Minor Works.* Translated by W.C. McDermott (Philadelphia, 1949), pp. 14-
15. (Preface to "The Glory of the Blessed Martyrs.")

seat of the eternal Judge, and was bound and lashed severely as a punishment, because too often he read the clever arguments of Cicero and the false tales of Virgil; and that in the presence of the sacred angels he confessed to the Lord of All that he would never henceforth read or discuss anything except that which was judged worthy of God. . . . Therefore we ought to pursue, to write, to speak, that which builds the church of God and by sacred teaching enriches needy minds by the knowledge of perfect faith. For we ought not to recall the lying stories, or to follow the wisdom of the philosophers which is hostile to God, lest we fall under the judgment of eternal death by the decision of the Lord. . . . I do not recall in my work the flight of Saturn, the wrath of Juno, the adulteries of Jupiter, the wrongdoings of Neptune, the scepter of Aeolus, the wars, the shipwreck, and the conquests of Aeneas. . . . I will describe neither the appearance of the Eumenides and various monsters nor the other fabulous stories which this author [Virgil] mendaciously invented or depicted in heroic verse. Having glanced at all these events built on sand and soon to perish, we return rather to divine and evangelical miracles.

— Reading No. 4 —

ASCENT OF THE CAROLINGIAN HOUSE

Reading 4A is taken from Einhard's famous Life of Charles the Great. *It contains the classic description of the life of the Merovingian puppet kings styled by the French* les rois fainéants *(do-nothing-kings), a description that in one form or another went into innumerable textbooks. The description is certainly exact. The Carolingians had long been the actual rulers. Still there was something about the ancient dynasty of the Merovingians that was difficult to destroy and to replace. A special "magic virtue" attached to them not as individuals but as descendants of an ancient house that drew their right to rule from a heroic if not divine ancestor. Still living in the tradition of what was called kin—or blood—right (the Germanic* Geblütsrecht), *the people recognized in the long locks and beard of the Merovingian princes the unmistakable signs of royal birth and stock which singled them out from the ranks of the common "folk." In order to succeed them Pepin had to overcome an old weakening belief with another of greater actuality and freshness. He turned to the pope, whose authority as representative of God and St. Peter had just recently been established in the mind of the people through the long labors of St. Boniface and his helpers. The anointment with the sacred oil and the blessings of the pope could serve as antidote against the old belief in the magic virtues of decaying royal blood. It is from the Royal Annals that we draw the report about Pepin's mission to Rome (4B). The question and answer as rendered here might be the annalist's own version. But there can be no doubt about the authenticity of the underlying meaning.*

✦ ✦ ✦

A. *From Einhard's* Life of Charlemagne[1]

1. The race of the Merovingians from which the Franks were accustomed to choose their kings is reckoned as lasting to King Hilderich [King Childeric III, 743-752], who, by the order of Stephen, the Roman pontiff, was deposed, tonsured, and sent into a monastery. But this race, though it may be regarded as finishing with him, had long since lost all power, and no longer possessed anything of importance except the empty royal title. For the wealth and power of the kingdom was in the hands of the Prae-fects of the Court, who were called Mayors of the Palace, and exercised entire sovereignty. The king, contented with the mere royal title, with long hair and flowing beard, used to sit upon the throne and act the part of a ruler, listening to ambassadors, whencesoever they came, and giving them at their departure as though of his own power, answers which he had been instructed or commanded to give. But this was the only function that he performed, for besides the empty royal title and the precarious life income which the Praefect of the Court allowed him at his pleasure he had nothing of his own except one estate with a very small revenue, on which he had his house, and from which he drew the few servants who performed such services as were necessary and made him a show of defer-ence. Wherever he had to go he travelled in a wagon, drawn in rustic style by a pair of oxen, and driven by a cowherd. In this fashion he used to go to the palace and to the general meetings of the people which were held yearly for the affairs of the kingdom; in this fashion he returned home. But the Praefect of the Court looked after the administration of the kingdom and all that had to be done or arranged at home or abroad.

2. When Hilderich was deposed, Pepin, the father of King Charles, was performing the duties of Mayor of the Palace as if by hereditary right. For his father Charles [Martel] . . . had served with distinction in the same office bequeathed to him by his own father. This honor is customarily given by the people only to those who excel others in nobility of birth and in amount of riches.

[1] From *Early Lives of Charlemagne* by Eginhard and the Monk of St. Gall. Translated and edited by A. J. Grant (London, 1926), pp. 8-9.

B. *From the* Royal Annals[1]

A.D. 749: Burghard, bishop of Würzburg, and the chaplain Fulrad were sent to Pope Zacharias to ask him about the kings in Francia. Since at that time they had no regal power: was this as it ought to be or was it not? And Pope Zacharias sent his answer to Pepin: that it would be better to call king the one who held the power rather than the one who remained without regal power. To keep the order undisturbed the Pope then ordered by virtue of his apostolic authority that Pepin should be crowned King.

— Reading No. 5 —

DONATIONS TO THE ROMAN CHURCH

The historian dealing with the "Donations" of the Carolingian princes to the See of St. Peter and the relationships between the popes and the kings created on account of them faces problems of criticism and interpretation which are among the most controversial in medieval history. For one thing, none of the documents that gave legal validity to promises and agreements has come down to us in the original. All we have are later "confirmations" of these documents by German kings and reports none too reliable because biased in favor of papal claims included in biographies (Vitae) of the respective popes. Of some help for the historian are references to the Donations in contemporary chronicles and, above all, the letters of the popes written to the Carolingian princes in the crucial

[1] Translated by H.W. from the *Annales regni Francorum (Laurissenses)* a. 749 (*Mon. Germ. Hist., Scriptores* I), p.137.

*period, 755-790. These letters were collected upon the
order of Charles himself in the so called* Codex Carolinus.

*Because of the difficulties of interpretation, a few re-
marks on the questions referred to in the documents of
this Reading are indicated. As regards the report in the
life of Pope Stephen II on the events at Ponthion and
Kiersy* (5A) *it is likely that the result of the agreement
made by Pepin with the pope was not a "charter of donation" which in the language of the time implies a grant of
objects (lands, rights) of which the donor holds possession
but a somewhat vague "promise" with at least some of the
objects undefined. Before he could "donate" Pepin had to
establish possession by victory and treaty with his Lombard enemies. New agreements were therefore concluded
between Pepin and Pope Stephen probably in 755* (5B)
*but most certainly in 756 after the second surrender of
the Lombard king Aistulf to Pepin* (5C). *In this charter
of donation, which the writer of the Life of Stephen
describes "as still to be found in the archives" of the
Church of St. Peter, Pepin donated or "restored" to the
pope the formerly Byzantine provinces of Ravenna and
of the Pentapolis once conquered by the Lombards from
the Byzantines and now conquered by himself for the See
of St. Peter. The charter must also have contained Pepin's
recognition and confirmation of the pope's jurisdiction
over the Roman Republic (see the "Promise" of Ponthion,
Reading 5A), that is, the Byzantine Duchy of Rome. Ever
since the extinction of the Byzantine dukedom of Rome
the popes had in fact acted as political leaders of "the
Romans" in their stead.*

*The "Donation" of 756 as described in 5C in all its
details and symbolic realization must, indeed, be considered as the action that brought the Papal States into
being. As for the term "restitution," the popes could have
used it legitimately only with respect to the estates of the
Church belonging to the so called Patrimony of St. Peter
in the above-mentioned provinces. But what the pope
now wanted was not only political control and jurisdiction
over the Romans of the duchy of Rome but also "the
rights and places" in the other two Byzantine provinces
with complete disregard of the historic position of the
Emperors in their Italian subkingdom. For papal sover-*

eignty no precedent or title could be found except perhaps in the "Donation of Constantine," which, as some scholars think, was fabricated to be presented to Pepin perhaps as early as 754 at Ponthion (5F). *In any case, it was as the political leader of Rome and the Romans that one pope bestowed upon Pepin the title* Patricius Romanarum *and another upon Charles the dignity of a Roman emperor.*

Another controversy is attached to the Confirmation of his father's Donations by Charlemagne in 774 (5D). *The Italian territory here described as Pepin's Donation at Kiersy far exceeds in extent the Byzantine provinces "restored" to Pope Stephen. If realized, the pope would have been given control over great parts of Lombard Italy. But this question is merely theoretical since, shortly after, Charlemagne conquered the Lombard kingdom for himself and his heirs. As king of the Lombards he was not interested in granting the popes Lombard territories. Only reluctantly did he make some territorial concessions to the popes later on to round off the territory of the former duchy of Rome with southern Tuscany, with some cities in the north of the duchy of Beneventum, and with the Sabina* (5E).

✓   ✓   ✓

A. *Pepin's "Promises" at Ponthion and Kiersy, 754* [1]

There [in Ponthion] . . . the most blessed pope [Stephen II] tearfully entreated the aforementioned Christian king [Pepin] to help the cause of St. Peter and of the Republic of the Romans by the conclusion of a peace treaty. The king immediately satisfied the most blessed pope under oath that he would do his best to obey all his orders and admonishments and according to the pope's will would return to him the Exarchate of Ravenna and the rights and places of the Republic by all means possible. . . . Then Pepin was absolved by the admonishments, blessings and prayers of the venerable pontiff and went to Kiersy. There he convened all the great men of

[1] Translated by H.W. from the *Vita Stephani II* in J. Haller, *Die Quellen zur Geschichte des Kirchenstaates* (Leipzig-Berlin, 1906), pp. 19-20.

his kingdom and conveying to them the holy admonishments of the pope together with them he decided to carry out, Christ helping, the agreements just made with the most blessed pope.

B. *Pope Stephen II Writes to Pepin and His Sons Complaining about the Failure of the Lombards to Keep Their Promises, 755* [1]

Our heart is saddened with great grief and our mind is depressed by the many tribulations we have suffered from the wickedness of Aistulf, king of the Lombards. We must refrain from wasting words and we try to inform your Christian excellency on one urgent matter. . . . Since God from heaven above mercifully granted you victories you attempted to gratify blessed Peter by confirming the restitution by a charter of Donation (*per donationis paginam*)[2]. . . . But the devil, that ancient enemy of mankind, entered his [Aistulf's] heart so that he seems to have gone back on his decision confirmed by sacred oaths. He has not allowed so much as one single handful of earth to be returned to blessed Peter and to the holy Church of God. . . .

C. *A Byzantine Interlude at Pavia, 756. The "Donation" of 756 and Its First Implementation by Abbot Fulrad of St. Denis*[3]

At the time when the aforementioned Pepin, most Christian king of the Franks, approached the *clusae* of the Lombards [the valley of Susa at the foot of Mont Cenis] two imperial messengers, the first secretary Georges, and the privy counselor Johannes, arrived in

[1] From *Codex Carolinus* no. 6, Haller, *loc. cit.*, pp. 82-83.
[2] E. Caspar, a scholar who has contributed much to the clarification of the problems connected with the "Donations," believes that the "page of donation" refers to the promise made by Pepin at Kiersy, 754. But there is more evidence in favor of the argument of W. Levison, J. Haller, and others who believe that it refers to a donation granted by Pepin to Pope Hadrian at the time of Pepin's first treaty with Aistulf at Pavia, 755.
[3] From the *Vita Stephani II*, Haller, *loc. cit.*, pp. 24-25.

this city of Rome with a message for the king of the
Franks. . . . [Later] one of them . . . followed the most
Christian king of the Franks and found him not far from
the city of Pavia within the lands of the Lombards. Here
he implored him urgently and with the promise of many
imperial gifts to surrender the city of Ravenna and other
cities and castles of the Exarchate to imperial officials; but
he was not able to persuade Pepin . . . to change his
mind. . . . This pious and generous king refused stead-
fastly to alienate these cities from the control of St. Peter,
from the jurisdiction of the Roman Church and from the
pontiff of the apostolic see; he confirmed under oath that
he had not engaged in frequent fighting for the sake of
man but for the love of St. Peter and the remission of his
sins. . . . Now, after Pepin, king of the Franks, had be-
sieged and conquered the city of Pavia, Aistulf, this most
atrocious king of the Lombards, in order to gain Pepin's
forgiveness, announced to this king his willingness to surrender the cities listed in the treaty, an act he had formerly thought contemptible. . . . On securing all the
cities, Pepin had a document of donation drafted for the
perpetual possession of these cities by the blessed Peter,
the Holy Roman Church, and all the future pontiffs of
the apostolic see. This document is still to be found in the
archives of our Holy Church.

The same most Christian king of the Franks sent his
counselor Fulrad, the venerable abbot and presbyter, to
receive these same cities, while he himself returned hap-
pily with his armies to Frankland. The said Fulrad, venerable abbot and priest, together with the emissaries of
king Aistulf, entered each city of the Pentapolis and the
Emilia [Ravenna], accepted their surrender, and took hostages from among the first citizens of each of them. These
he dispatched to Rome together with the keys of the gates
of the cities. Then he deposited on the tomb of St. Peter
the keys of the city of Ravenna and of the various cities
of the Exarchate as well as the aforementioned document
of donation issued by the king by which the apostles of
God and his vicar, the most holy pope, and all the pontiffs
who succeeded him were to hold the cities perpetually.
These cities were Ravenna, etc. [there follows a long list
of cities of the Emilia and the Pentapolis]. . . .

D. *The Confirmation of the Donation of Pepin by Charles, King of the Franks and Lombards, on April 6, 774, in the Presence of Pope Hadrian*[1]

. . . But on the Wednesday of this week the pontiff accompanied by his officials, both ecclesiastical and military, met the king in the church of St. Peter for a parley. He urgently beseeched the king . . . to fulfill all points of the promises given by his father Pepin of blessed memory, the late king, and by Charles himself and his brother Carloman and all the Frankish magnates to Pope Stephen II, at the time he went to Frankland, to grant the various cities and territories of that Italian province and to surrender them to the blessed Peter and all his vicars in perpetual possession. When he had the promise of Kiersy read to him, Charles and his magnates liked it and also approved of the additions. And out of his free will the most excellent and most Christian king of the Franks, Charles, had a new promise of donation on the model of the earlier one written down by his chaplain and secretary Etherius wherein he confirmed to the blessed Peter the same cities and territories and pledged himself to surrender them to the said pontiff within the confines contained in that donation.[2] . . . This donation was first deposited on the altar of St. Peter and later below [inside?] in the confession. . . .

E. *A Letter Concerning the Donation of 781: Pope Hadrian Admonishes King Charles to Carry out his Promise of Surrendering the Sabina to the Pope*[3]

To our most excellent son and spiritual common father with ourselves, the lord Charles, king of the Franks and Lombards and patricius of the Romans, Pope Hadrian. . . . When our and your most faithful messengers . . .

---

[1] *Ibid.,* pp. 54-55.

[2] In the passage that follows, the region described contains large parts of Italy from the northern coast of the Tyrrhenian Sea including the island of Corsica to the Adriatic, "the whole exarchate of Ravenna as it was of old," Venetia and Istria and the Lombard Duchies of Spoleto and Beneventum.

[3] From the *Codex Carolinus* (no. 71), Haller, *loc. cit.,* p. 205.

went to the territory of the Sabina [in the southeast corner of the duchy of Rome] to carry out the surrender of this whole territory according to your kind dispositions they were not able to do so since wicked men put obstacles in their way. . . . Therefore we dispatched to your royal and God-pleasing Highness our messenger Stephanus, our long time treasurer, to suggest that for the sake of your soul you order the whole mentioned territory of the Sabina to be surrendered to the blessed Peter, keyholder to the kingdom of Heaven, as you have started doing. . . .

F. *The "Donation of Constantine," a Forgery of the Second Part of the Eighth Century*[1]

The forged Decree of Emperor Constantine (*called* Constitutum Constantini) *was inserted in a legendary biography of Pope Sylvester I* (*314-335*). *Though it is admittedly a forgery connected with the papal territorial aspirations of the latter part of the eighth century scholars still disagree about the exact date. The administration of Paul I* (*757-768*) *seems the best possibility. The core of the* Vita Silvestri *is the story of how the emperor was stricken with leprosy, how he was cured of it by the miraculous intervention of Pope Sylvester I, how he was baptized by the pope and how, to show his gratitude to the pope and the Church, he issued a Decree of Donation. From this decree we give here the paragraphs referring to certain claims of the papacy to imperial precedence and to the rule over Italy:*

14. . . . Therefore we grant and with this present decree convey to the same holy apostles, my lords, the most blessed Peter and Paul, and through them to the blessed Sylvester, our father, supreme pontiff and universal pope of the city of Rome, and to all their successors who to the end of the world will sit in the see of St. Peter, our imperial palace of the Lateran which is supreme over all the palaces of the earth; furthermore our imperial diadem or crown together with the mitre (*frygium*) and the

[1] Translated by H. W. from K. Mirbt, *Quellen zur Geschichte des Papsttums und des Römischen Katholizismus* (Tübingen, 1934), no. 228, pp. 111-112.

shoulder stole, which encircles our imperial neck as well as the purple cloak and the scarlet tunic and the whole imperial attire and the command of the imperial cavalry. . . .

17. Also, to match the greatness of the empire and not to debase the pontifical apex but to adorn its dignity which is higher than that of a terrestrial empire, and the might of its glory, we convey and surrender to the often mentioned most blessed pontiff, our father Sylvester, the universal pope, and to the power and jurisdiction of the pontiffs, his successors, not only our palace as mentioned before but also all the provinces, places and districts of the city of Rome,[1] of Italy and the regions of the West . . . as a legal and permanent possession of the Roman Church.

— Reading No. 6 —

CONVERSION OF THE SAXONS

The desperate efforts of Charlemagne to subjugate the Saxons by putting an end to their rebellions are reflected in the Capitulary concerning the Saxons which is inserted in its entirety under 6A below. It cannot be dated exactly. some scholars connect it with the introduction in Saxony of the Frankish county system in 782, others with the

---

[1] This is a literal rendering of the grammatical construction found in the best manuscripts on which the text is based (K. Zeumer). The translation above is in agreement with those of R. Laffan, *Select Historical Documents* (New York, 1929), p. 5, and H. Bettenson, *Documents of the Christian Church* (Oxford, 1942), p. 141, whereas C. Coleman makes *city of Rome* direct object, and it is this version that found its way into textbooks.

*conquest of the Saxons and the surrender and baptism of
their popular leader Widukind in 785.*

*An entirely unprecedented measure taken in this Capit-
ulary was the suspension of the old folk law of the Saxons
and its replacement by a kind of martial law. Death, for
instance, was now imposed for murder, a crime which
according to Germanic law customs would have been
"composed" by the payment of* wergeld *to the family of
the slain and to the king. Points 3-14 of the "major
chapters" below suggest that the Saxons were given no
other choice than that between conversion and death.
Points 15-34, the "lesser chapters," aim primarily at the
establishment of endowments for the new churches in
Saxony. Some of them imply Frankish infringement in the
free property of the Saxons. The prohibition against con-
vening the public assemblies of freemen except under order and authority of the* missi *struck at the root of the free
government of the Saxons. A mood of revenge and wrath
in the king rather than political wisdom seems to have
dictated these chapters. Nor did they escape criticism in
Charles's own time. Alcuin voiced it freely to the king and
his advisers in letters from which excerpts are given under
6B. It was perhaps due to his influence that after his warn-
ing had been substantiated by new wars and uprisings a
new capitulary was issued in 792 and another in 802
which mitigated some of the most severe articles and procedures of the earlier decree.*

✓   ✓   ✓

A. *Capitulatio de partibus Saxoniae*, 775-790 [1]

First, concerning the major chapters it has been enacted:

1. It was pleasing to all that the churches of Christ,
which are now being built in Saxony and consecrated to
God, should not have less, but greater and more illustrious
honor, than the fanes of the idols had had.

2. If any one shall have fled to a church for refuge,
let no one presume to expel him from the church by vio-

[1] University of Pennsylvania, *Translations and Reprints*, VI,
5, pp. 2-5.

lence, but he shall be left in peace until he shall be brought to the judicial assemblage; and on account of the honor due to God and the saints, and the reverence due to the church itself, let his life and all his members be granted to him. Moreover, let him plead his cause as best he can and he shall be judged; and so let him be led to the presence of the lord king, and the latter shall send him where it shall have seemed fitting to his clemency.

3. If any one shall have entered a church by violence and shall have carried off anything in it by force or theft, or shall have burned the church itself, let him be punished by death.

4. If any one, out of contempt for Christianity, shall have despised the holy Lenten fast and shall have eaten flesh, let him be punished by death. But, nevertheless, let it be taken into consideration by a priest, lest perchance any one from necessity has been led to eat flesh.

5. If any one shall have killed a bishop or priest or deacon, let him likewise be punished capitally.

6. If any one deceived by the devil shall have believed, after the manner of the pagans, that any man or woman is a witch and eats men, and on this account shall have burned the person, or shall have given the person's flesh to others to eat, or shall have eaten it himself, let him be punished by a capital sentence.

7. If any one, in accordance with pagan rites, shall have caused the body of a dead man to be burned and shall have reduced his bones to ashes, let him be punished capitally.

8. If any one of the race of the Saxons hereafter concealed among them shall have wished to hide himself unbaptized, and shall have scorned to come to baptism and shall have wished to remain a pagan, let him be punished by death.

9. If any one shall have sacrificed a man to the devil, and after the manner of the pagans shall have presented him as a victim to the demons, let him be punished by death.

10. If any one shall have formed a conspiracy with the pagans against the Christians, or shall have wished to join with them in opposition to the Christians, let him be

punished by death; and whoever shall have consented to this same fraudulently against the king and the Christian people, let him be punished by death.

11. If any one shall have shown himself unfaithful to the lord king, let him be punished with a capital sentence.

12. If any one shall have ravished the daughter of his lord, let him be punished by death.

13. If any one shall have killed his lord or lady, let him be punished in a like manner.

14. If, indeed, for these mortal crimes secretly committed any one shall have fled of his own accord to a priest, and after confession shall have wished to do penance, let him be freed by the testimony of the priest from death.

15. Concerning the lesser chapter all have consented. To each church let the parishioners present a house and two mansi of land, and for each one hundred and twenty men, noble and free, and likewise liti [freedmen], let them give to the same church a man-servant and a maid-servant.

16. And this has been pleasing, Christ being propitious, that whencesoever any receipts shall have come into the treasury, either for a breach of the peace or for any penalty of any kind, and in all income pertaining to the king, a tithe shall be rendered to the churches and priests.

17. Likewise, in accordance with the mandate of God, we command that all shall give a tithe of their property and labor to the churches and priests; let the nobles as well as the freemen, and likewise the liti, according to that which God shall have given to each Christian, return a part to God.

18. That on the Lord's day no meetings and public judicial assemblages shall be held, unless perchance in a case of great necessity or when war compels it, but all shall go to the church to hear the word of God, and shall be free for prayers or good works. Likewise, also, on the especial festivals they shall devote themselves to God and to the services of the church, and shall refrain from secular assemblies.

19. Likewise, it has been pleasing to insert in these decrees that all infants shall be baptized within a year; and we have decreed this, that if any one shall have despised to bring his infant to baptism within the course of

a year, without the advice or permission of the priest, if he is a noble he shall pay 120 solidi to the treasury, if a freeman 60, is a litus 30.

20. If any shall have made a prohibited or illegal marriage, if a noble 60 solidi, if a freeman 30, if a litus 15.

21. If any one shall have made a vow at springs or trees or groves, or shall have made any offerings after the manner of the heathen and shall have partaken of a repast in honor of the demons, if he shall be a noble 60 solidi, if a freeman 30, if a litus 15. If, indeed they have not the means of paying at once, they shall be given into the service of the church until the solidi are paid.

22. We command that the bodies of Saxon Christians shall be carried to the church cemeteries and not to the mounds of the pagans.

23. We have ordered that diviners and soothsayers shall be given to the church and priests.

33. Concerning perjuries, let it be according to the law of the Saxons.[1]

34. We have forbidden that all the Saxons shall hold public assemblies in general, unless perchance our *missus* shall have caused them to come together in accordance with our command; but each count shall hold judicial assemblies and administer justice in his jurisdiction. And this shall be cared for by the priests, lest it be done otherwise.

B. *From Alcuin's Letters to Bishop Arn of Salzburg, King Charles and His Chamberlain Meginfred on Moderation to be Used toward the Newly Conquered Saxons, 796* [2]

1. To Arn of Salzburg:

Be a preacher of piety rather than a collector of tithes: for an untutored soul has to be nurtured gradually on the milk of apostolic piety until it grows and becomes healthy and strong enough to digest more solid food. People say that the tithes have undermined the faith of the Saxons.

[1] Death penalty.
[2] Translated by H.W. from *Alcuini Epistolae* (*Mon. Germ. Hist., Epistolae* IV), nos. 107, 113, 110, 111, pp. 154, 164, 158, 161.

Should one impose on the neck of the ignorant a yoke that neither ourselves nor our brethren have been able to bear? Therefore we believe that the souls of the faithful are to be saved by faith in Christ.

2. To the same:

The whole miserable race of the Saxons have lost the benefit of baptism because they have never really received in their heart the fundamentals of faith. It should also be known that according to Saint Augustine faith is an act of the will and cannot be enforced. . . . A man can be forced into accepting baptism but not faith. . . .

3. To King Charles:

Your Holy Piety may also consider the following: is it really good to impose on barbarians, who have just recently been introduced to the Christian faith, the full burden of the tithes, that is to collect it from every single house? Would it not be better to consider the attitude of the apostles . . . as regards the exacting of tithes from everybody? We know that payment of tithes from our property is a very good thing but it is better to forego it than to ruin the faith of the Saxons. . . . Careful consideration should also be given to the proper order of preaching and the dispensation of sacraments: for little benefit will accrue to the body by the ablutions of sacred baptism unless the soul has first accepted the truth of the Catholic faith on rational grounds. . . .

4. To Charles' chamberlain Meginfred:

If the light yoke and sweet burden of Christ were preached to the most stubborn Saxons with as much zeal as we show in our effort to enforce the tithe or to exact the legally presented penalty for misdemeanors, however trifling, perhaps they would not be so reluctant to accept the sacrament of baptism. . . .

RONCESVALLES

At first, the defeat suffered by Charlemagne's rear guard at Roncesvalles was passed over in silence by the writers contemporary with the event. Only the author of the Royal Annals *mentioned it, but without giving any details. Later, Einhard inserted in his* Life of Charlemagne *what seems to be a fairly accurate account of the event, reproduced here. He also mentioned the names of three leaders, among them Roland, "praefect of the Bretons." But nothing in the story he tells suggests the heroic role that the Breton count was to play in the later chanson de geste that bears his name or in the legendary cycle that revolves around Charlemagne and his paladins. The defeat may not even have been as disastrous as the legend has it. Great importance was attached to it later, at the time of the First Crusade, when the Chanson de Roland was probably composed. The story of the defeat suffered on the return from an expedition against the infidels in Spain could easily be converted into one where it was inflicted upon the Christians by the Saracens themselves.*

✓   ✓   ✓

Einhard's Account[1]

While the war with the Saxons was being prosecuted constantly and almost continuously he placed garrisons at suitable places on the frontier, and attacked Spain with the largest military expedition that he could collect. He crossed the Pyrenees, received the surrender of all the towns and fortresses that he attacked, and returned with his army safe and sound, except for a reverse which he experienced through the treason of the Gascons on his return through the passes of the Pyrenees. For while his

[1] From *Early Lives of Charlemagne* . . . translated by A. J. Grant (London, 1926), pp. 19-20.

army was marching in a long line, suiting their formation to the character of the ground and the defiles, the Gascons placed an ambuscade on the top of the mountain—where the density and extent of the woods in the neighbourhood rendered it highly suitable for such a purpose—and then rushing down into the valley beneath threw into disorder the last part of the baggage train and also the rear guard which acted as a protection to those in advance. In the battle which followed the Gascons slew their opponents to the last man. Then they seized upon the baggage, and under cover of the night, which was already falling, they scattered with the utmost rapidity in different directions. The Gascons were assisted in this feat by the lightness of their armour and the character of the ground where the affair took place. In this battle Eggihard, the surveyor of the royal table, Anselm, the Count of the Palace, and Roland, Praefect of the Breton frontier, were killed along with many others. Nor could this assault be punished at once, for when the deed had been done the enemy so completely disappeared that they left behind them not so much as a rumour of their whereabouts.

— Reading No. 8 —

CORONATION OF CHARLEMAGNE

For the evaluation of the events that led to the momentous coronation at St. Peter's the letters written by Charles and his advisers in the years preceding it provide important information. They are especially informative as to Charles's ideas about the king's role within the Church and his intention to extend royal leadership and supervision to all ecclesiastical matters, not excluding the moral and religious behavior of the pope himself. Excerpts from

Charles's instruction to Abbot Angilbert of St. Riquier, whom he sent to Rome as his special messenger immediately after the coronation of the new Pope Leo III, as well as excerpts from a letter of congratulation which Angilbert was to deliver to the pope demonstrate clearly this point (8A, 8B). In the years following Angilbert's mission to Rome the events that forced Leo to seek the protection of the Frankish king in Germany further strengthened the belief of the king and his entourage that the Frankish king was commissioned by God to restore the peace of the Church and the welfare of Christianity. This point is made emphatically in a letter written by Alcuin to King Charles just half a year before the coronation (8C), a fact interpreted by historians as a proof that the idea of exalting the Frankish king to imperial dignity originated among Charles's scholars at his court in Aachen.

As regards the coronation itself, contemporary reports do not attribute too much importance to it; they are rather sparse in details. The one found in the Royal Annals (8D) is probably closest to the events, whereas the report of the annalist of Lorsch (8E) is interesting because of his attempt to justify Charles's acceptance of the imperial title before the Byzantines, an attempt which we also find in Einhard (8H). The official report of the Roman Church was inserted in The Life of Pope Leo (8F). A brief statement consisting of one sentence only, found in the Chronography of the Byzantine Theophanes (8G), possibly suggests the contempt of the author for the foolish act of a royal usurper and his papal puppet. Finally, Einhard's account of the coronation (8H) is the only one to refer to the coronation ceremony as a surprise to which the new emperor reacted in a rather negative way.

✦   ✦   ✦

A. *Charles to Abbot Angilbert of St. Riquier, Instructing Him How to Admonish Pope Leo III*, 796 [1]

May the mercy of God lead you safely and prosperously to our father, the apostolic Lord. Admonish him diligently to live honestly and to give special attention to observing

[1] Translated by H.W. from *Epistolae Alcuini* (*Mon. Germ. Hist., Epistolae* IV), no. 92, pp. 135-136.

126 THE ERA OF CHARLEMAGNETHE ERA OF CHARLEMAGNE

the holy canons; tell him he ought to govern the Holy Church of God in the spirit of piety according to the agreement to be reached between him and you and according to his own light. Tell him frequently how transitory the honor is which he has received recently as against the eternal reward to be given to one who labors toward this end. Advise him to apply himself diligently to the repression of the heresy of simony, for this harms the body of the Church in many ways, and tell him whatever you recall of the problems you and I have discussed between ourselves. . . . The Lord God guide you and bring you back safely. The Lord God may guide and direct his heart [the pope's] in every goodness so that he may serve his Holy Church, may lead us as our pious father, and intervene in our behalf.

B. *From a Letter Written by King Charles to Pope Leo Congratulating Him upon his Election to the Papacy, 796* [1]

In order to confirm our peaceful concord we are dispatching our faithful adviser and secretary Angilbert to your holiness. . . . To him we have given full instructions regarding our wishes and your requirements. In your interchange of views you may treat whatever you consider necessary for the exaltation of God's Holy Church, for the firm foundation of your honor, or for the strengthening of our Patriciate. . . .

*There follows the famous statement about the collaboration between the secular and spiritual powers and the different tasks assigned to each (see below, Reading No. 16*B*).*

. . . Let your prudence always pay attention to the precepts of the canons . . . so that your life in every way may serve as an example of holiness. . . .

C. From a Letter by Alcuin to King Charles (whom he calls *David Rex*) on "the Three Highest Powers in this World," June 799 [2]

[1] *Ibid.,* no. 93, pp. 137-138.
[2] *Ibid.,* no. 174, p. 288.

To this day three persons have held the highest positions in this world: The apostolic sublimity who as the vicar of the blessed Peter, prince of the apostles, occupies his see. Thanks to your care I have been informed of the fate of the last incumbent of this see. The second is the imperial dignity and the secular power of the Second Rome. The rumor of the impious fashion in which the present head of the empire was deposed not by foreigners but by relatives and fellow citizens has spread everywhere. The third person is the royal dignity to the peak of which you have been exalted as the ruler of the Christian people: it excels the two others in power, renown for wisdom, and sublime royal dignity. The welfare of the Church is now in danger and rests on you alone: you are the avenger of evil deeds, the guide of those who go astray, the comforter of those who mourn, the glory of the good. . . .

D. *From the* Frankish Royal Annals, December 25, 800 [1]

On that very holy day of the nativity of the Lord when the king, at mass before the tomb of the blessed apostle Peter, arose from prayer, Pope Leo placed upon his head a crown and the whole Roman people acclaimed him: Life and victory to Charles, Augustus, crowned by God, the great and peaceful Emperor of the Romans! And after the laudation he was adored by the pope in the manner of ancient princes and instead of Patricius he was now titled Emperor and Augustus.

E. *From the* Annals of Lorsch[2], 801

And as the title of an emperor had then come to an end among the Greeks, since they had a woman on the imperial throne, it seemed to Pope Leo and the holy fathers assembled at the council as well as to the rest of the Christian people that they should give the title of emperor to Charles, king of the Franks, since he held not only

---

[1] Translated by H.W. from the *Annales regni Francorum ad a.*801 (Hannover, 1896), p. 112.
[2] Translated by H.W. from the *Annales Laureshamenses* (*Mon. Germ. Hist., Scriptores* I), p. 38.

Rome itself, where the Caesars used to reside, but the other seats in Italy, Gaul, and Germany as well. Since the almighty God had given into his possession all these places, they deemed it right that with the assistance of God and according to the request of the whole Christian people he should bear the title also. King Charles was not able to refuse this demand: in all humility he submitted to God and to the request of the whole Christian people and on the day of the nativity of our Lord Jesus Christ he assumed the title of an emperor and was consecrated by Pope Leo.

F. *From the* Life of Pope Leo[1]

23. After this [the purgation oath of Leo taken in the Basilica of St. Peter] all convened again on the day of the nativity in the above-mentioned Basilica of the blessed apostle Peter. And then the venerable and peaceful pontiff crowned him with his own hands with that most precious crown. Then all the faithful Romans who saw how he was eager to defend and how he loved the Holy Roman Church and its vicar, cried out with one voice—and this was the will of God and of the blessed Peter, the keyholder to the kingdom of heaven: To Charles, the most pious Augustus, crowned by God, the great and peaceful emperor, life and victory! This was announced three times before the holy confession of the Blessed Apostle Peter while they were invoking various saints; and he was established by all as Emperor of the Romans. 24. Thereupon the most holy prelate and pontiff anointed king Charles, his most excellent son, with the holy oil on that very day of the nativity of our Lord Jesus Christ.

G. *From Theophanes'* Chronicle[2]

In this year in the month of December Charles, the king of the Franks, was crowned by Pope Leo.

---

[1] Translated by H.W. from *Vita Leonis, Liber Pontificalis* (ed. L. Duchesne, Vol. I, Paris, 1886), II, 7.
[2] From *Theophanes, Chronographia*, A.M. 6293, Migne, *Patrologiae cursus completus, Series Graeca*, CVIII, col. 956.

H. *From Einhard,* Life of Charlemagne[1]

27. Although he held it [the Roman Church] in great respect, he only traveled to Rome to fulfil his vows and make his supplications four times during the forty-seven years of his reign.

28. But for his last journey there was still another reason. The Romans had inflicted many injuries upon Pope Leo, tearing out his eyes and cutting out his tongue[2] so that he felt compelled to implore the help of the king. Therefore he went to Rome to restore order in the much disturbed affairs of the Church, and stayed there for the whole winter. At this time he received the titles of Emperor and Augustus. But at first he disliked this act so much that he declared that, had he anticipated the intention of the pontiff, he would not have entered the church on that day when it happened, although it was a great feast day. But he endured very patiently the jealousy of the emperors who were indignant about his assuming these titles. By sending them frequent embassies and letters in which he addressed them as brothers, he overcame their contempt with his magnanimity, in which he was undoubtedly their superior.

[1] Translated by H. W. from *Vita Caroli Magni,* ed. G. Waitz (Hannover, 1911), p. 32.
[2] But see above, p. 41, note.

BYZANTINE RECOGNITION OF CHARLEMAGNE

After his coronation Charlemagne was able to impose on all his subjects the oath of fidelity to him as an emperor (see Reading No. 12). But he met with the greatest difficulties when he tried to gain the much-sought-for recognition of his new dignity from the emperor in Constantinople. After an honest attempt to come to terms with the emperor Nikephoros had failed, Charles and his son Pepin, king of Italy, were forced to wage a war which dragged on for years. The odds were finally in favor of Pepin—he had forced Venice and places along the Dalmatian coast to capitulate—when the emperor decided to sue for peace (811). Charles, who later confessed to have waited seven years for this occasion, invited the Byzantine delegation to appear at his palace in Aachen. He then solemnly renounced all the conquests, including Venice, in return for the official recognition by his eastern "senior": the Byzantine delegation hailed him as Emperor and Basileus (9A). In a letter written shortly after, Charlemagne expressed his rejoicing over this achievement. To judge from the terms in the letter the thought of the price he paid for it seemed not to have bothered him much (9B). What he envisaged bringing about was a world equally partitioned between the oriental and occidental empires, at peace with each other because united in the Christian faith. Charlemagne's decision to give up concrete advantages and objectives for a dignity and a title was certainly not a credit to his statesmanship. But in this he was by no means unique among medieval rulers, including many who bore the imperial crown as his successors.

✶   ✶   ✶

A. *The Conclusion of Peace According to the* Annals of Lorsch, 812 [1]

. . . After he had won many brilliant victories in Moesia the Emperor Nikephoros was killed in a battle against the Bulgars, and his son-in-law Michael was made emperor. It was Michael who received in Constantinople the ambassadors sent by Emperor Charles to Nikephoros and who dispatched them back to Aachen along with his own delegates, the Bishop Michael and the protospatharii Arsafius and Theognostus. They were commissioned to conclude the peace initiated by Nikephoros. After their arrival at the emperor's court in Aachen they received from his hands the peace treaty in the palace church and then they hailed him (*laudes ei dixerunt*) in their own fashion, that is in the Greek [ritual and] language, as Emperor and Basileus. On their return trip they stopped in Rome and received in the Basilica of St. Peter the Apostle another copy of the peace treaty [signed] by Pope Leo.

B. *From a Letter of Charlemagne*, 813 [2]

We praise our Lord Jesus Christ, our true God, and give thanks to Him with all the strength of our body and mind and with all our heart: for with His unfathomable goodness He made us worthy to establish in our own days the long desired and longed for peace between the Western and Eastern Empires. He also permitted us always to rule and to protect according to her daily needs His holy and immaculate Catholic Church (*ecclesia*) which is spread throughout the world, and even now He has granted it to us to unify and pacify her in our own time. . . .

[1] Translated by H.W. from *Annales Laurissenses vel Einhardi* (*Mon. Germ. Hist., Scriptores* I), p. 199.
[2] Translated by H.W. from *Epistolae variorum* (*Mon. Germ. Hist., Epistolae* IV), no. 37, p. 556.

ECONOMIC ORGANIZATION

*As an example of the economic organization of Charle-
magne's fiscal estates (or any manorial estate of the age)
we include in this Reading (10A) excerpts from Charlemagne's famous* Capitulare de Villis *in the order introduced by the English translator, that is, with the general
instruction for the manorial officials as to the drawing up
of an inventory put at the beginning. As a counterpart
these excerpts are followed (10B) by an example of an
inventory drawn up in line with these instructions. The
inventory is from an estate called Asnapium, a place that
scholars so far have not been able to locate. It must have
been a rather small place with not much specialization in
crafts and services represented. It is likely that such de-
ficiencies as the lack of a blacksmith, swordmaker, etc.,
were supplemented from nearby fiscal estates. This would
bear out the assumption that self-sufficiency was not the
rule within one manorial unit but rather within groups of
estates belonging to a lord, and there were always goods
like iron and salt that had to be imported from outside.
Clause 45 of the* Capitulare de Villis *implies that the raw
material required for the numerous crafts were imported.
As to the manner of consumption we hear very little. In
Clause 44 of the Capitulary, Charles orders the steward
to send part of the food products "each year for our own
use," that is, to his temporary or permanent residence.*

✓   ✓   ✓

A. *Articles from the Capitulary* "De Villis" [1]

62. That each steward shall make an annual statement
of all our income: an account of our lands cultivated by
the oxen which our ploughmen drive and of our lands

[1] From University of Pennsylvania, *Translations and Reprints,*
III, 2, pp. 2-4.

which the tenants of farms ought to plough; an account of
the pigs, of the rents, of the obligations and fines; of the
game taken in our forests without our permission; of the
various compositions; of the mills, of the forest, of
the fields, of the bridges, and ships: of the free-men and
the hundreds who are under obligations to our treasury;
of markets, vineyards, and those who owe wine to us; of
the hay, fire-wood, torches, planks, and other kinds of lum-
ber; of the wasteland; of the vegetables, millet, panic; of
the wool, flax, and hemp; of the fruits of the trees, of the
nut trees, larger and smaller; of the grafted trees of all
kinds; of the gardens; of the turnips; of the fish-ponds;
of the hides, skins, and horns; of the honey, wax; of the
fat, tallow and soap; of the mulberry wine, cooked wine,
mead, vinegar, beer, wine new and old; of the new grain
and the old; of the hens and eggs; of the geese; the number of fishermen, smiths [workers in metal], sword-makers,
and shoe-makers; of the bins and boxes; of the turners and
saddlers; of the forges and mines, that is iron and other
mines; of the lead mines; of the tributaries; of the colts
and fillies; they shall make all these known to us, set forth
separately and in order, at Christmas, in order that we
may know what and how much of each thing we have.

22. In each of our estates our stewards are to have as
many cow-houses, piggeries, sheep-folds, stables for goats,
as possible, and they ought never to be without these. And
let them have in addition cows furnished by our serfs for
performing their service, so that the cow-houses and
plows shall be in no way weakened by the service on our
demesne. And when they have to provide meat, let them
have steers lame, but healthy, and cows and horses which
are not mangy, or other beasts which are not diseased and,
as we have said, our cow-houses and plows are not to be
weakened for this.

34. They must provide with the greatest care, that
whatever is prepared or made with the hands, that is,
lard, smoked meat, salt meat, partially salted meat, wine,
vinegar, mulberry wine, cooked wine, garns,[1] mustard,
cheese, butter, malt, beet, mead, honey, wax, flour, all
should be prepared and made with the greatest cleanliness.

[1] A kind of fermented liquor.

40. That each steward on each of our domains shall always have, for the sake of ornament, swans, peacocks, pheasants, ducks, pigeons, partridges, turtle-doves.

42. That in each of our estates, the chambers shall be provided with counterpanes, cushions, pillows, bed-clothes, coverings for the tables and benches; vessels of brass, lead, iron and wood; andirons, chains, pot-hooks, adzes, axes, augers, cutlasses and all other kinds of tools, so that it shall never be necessary to go elsewhere for them, or to borrow them. And the weapons, which are carried against the enemy, shall be well cared for, so as to keep them in good condition; and when they are brought back they shall be placed in the chamber.

43. For our women's work they are to give at the proper time, as has been ordered, the materials, that is the linen, wool, woad, vermilion, madder, wool-combs, teasels, soap, grease, vessels and the other objects which are necessary.

44. Of the food-products other than meat, two-thirds shall be sent each year for our own use, that is of the vegetables, fish, cheese, butter, honey, mustard, vinegar, millet, panic, dried and green herbs, radishes, and in addition of the wax, soap and other small products; and they tell us how much is left by a statement, as we have said above; and they shall not neglect this as in the past; because from those two-thirds we wish to know how much remains.

45. That each steward shall have in his district good workmen, namely, blacksmiths, gold-smiths, silver-smiths, shoemakers, turners, carpenters, sword-makers, fishermen, foilers, soap-makers, men who know how to make beer, cider, berry, and all the other kinds of beverages, bakers to make pastry for our table, net-makers who know how to make nets for hunting, fishing, and fowling, and the other who are too numerous to be designated.

B. *Inventory of an Estate of Charles the Great*[1]

We found in the domain estate of Asnapium a royal house built of stone in the best manner, 3 rooms; the whole house surrounded with balconies, with 11 apart-

[1] *Ibid.,* pp. 4-5.

ments for women; beneath 1 cellar; 2 porticoes; 17 other houses built of wood within the court-yard with as many rooms and other appurtenances, well built; 1 stable, 1 kitchen, 1 mill, 1 granary, 3 barns.

The yard surrounded carefully with a hedge and stone gateway and above a balcony from which to make distributions. An inner yard, likewise enclosed within a hedge, arranged in a suitable manner planted with various kinds of trees.

Vestments: coverings for 1 bed, 1 table cloth, 1 towel.

Utensils: 2 brass kettles, 2 drinking cups, 2 brass cauldrons, 1 iron one, 1 frying-pan, 1 gramalmin, 1 pair of andirons, 1 lamp, 2 hatchets, 1 chisel, 2 augers, 1 axe, 1 knife, 1 large plate, 1 plate, 2 scythes, 2 sickels, 2 spades tipped with iron. Enough wooden utensils for use.

Farm produce: old spelt from last year, 90 baskets which can be made into 450 weights of flour; 100 measures of barley. From the present year, 110 baskets of spelt, planted 60 baskets from the same, the rest we found; 100 measures of wheat, 60 sown, the rest we found; 98 measures of rye all sown; 1800 measures of barley, 1100 sown, the rest we found; 430 measures of oats, 1 measure of beans, 12 measures of peas. At the 5 mills, 800 measures, small measures. At the 4 breweries, 650 measures, small measures, 240 given to the prebendaries, the rest we found. At the 2 bridges, 60 measures of salt and 2 shillings. At the 4 gardens, 11 shillings. Honey, 3 measures; about 1 measure of butter; lard, from last year 10 sides, new sides 200 with fragments and fats, cheese from the present year 43 weights.

Of cattle: 51 head of larger cattle, 5 three-year-olds, 7 two-year-olds, 7 yearlings; 10 two-year-old colts, 8 yearlings, 3 stallions; 16 cows; 2 asses; 50 cows with calves, 20 young bullocks, 38 yearling calves, 3 bulls, 260 hogs, 100 pigs, 5 boars, 150 sheep with lambs, 200 yearling lambs, 120 rams, 30 goats with kids, 30 yearling kids, 2 male goats, 30 geese, 80 chickens, 22 peacocks.

Also concerning the dependencies which pertain to the above mansion. In the villa of Grisio we found domain buildings, where there are 3 barns and a yard surrounded by a hedge. There is there 1 garden with trees, 10 geese, 8 ducks, 30 chickens.

In another villa. We found domain buildings and a yard surrounded by a hedge and within 3 barns, 1 arpent of vines, 1 garden with trees, 15 geese, 20 chickens.

In a third villa, domain buildings. It has 2 barns, 1 granary, 1 garden, 1 yard well enclosed by a hedge.

We found all the dry and liquid measures just as in the palace. We did not find any goldsmiths, silversmiths, blacksmiths, huntsmen, or persons engaged in other services.

The garden herbs which we found were lily, putchuck, mint, parsley, rue, celery, libesticum, sage, savory, juniper, leeks, garlic, tansy, wild mint, coriander, scullions, onions, cabbage, kohl-rabi, betony. Trees: pears, apples, medlars, peaches, filberts, walnuts, mulberries, quinces.

— Reading No. 11 —

MILITARY ORGANIZATION

The military organization of Charlemagne's empire was an outgrowth of conditions created by the Merovingian conquest of Gaul. To his tribal warriors who fought in his armies Clovis added the soldiers of the Roman general Syagrius whom he had conquered. Likewise, after the conquest of the Burgundians, he imposed upon them special military obligations. He also encouraged the Gallo-Romans in general to volunteer for military service. On their descendants, however, this service was then enforced as a hereditary duty. All the factors combined, including the pressure by the counts on the local freemen, the obligations of the "followers" toward their "great men" and those of horsemen toward lords from whom they had received benefices in the time of Charles Mariel worked toward making military service a hereditary duty of all freemen. Charlemagne exploited this situation to the utmost. All freemen were liable to military service for a number of months each year and at their own cost. In numerous capitularies he regulated to the most minute detail the services owed by the freemen as well as the punishments and penalties for failure to appear or to pay the tax in lieu of service called haribannus *(11A). Special attention is given in these capitularies to the equipment with victuals, arms and clothing; some include the prohibition of selling arms to enemies or even merely outside the realm. Although on principle the individual freeman was made responsible for the execution of the imperial orders we note the tendency to put the burden of responsibility on the local count or lord (11B and 11C). Because of the unceasing wars and military campaigns in which he was engaged, Charlemagne drew so heavily on the manpower and resources of his empire that he had to take special measures to prevent the complete impoverishment of the freeman class and a serious food shortage on an empire-wide scale (11C).*

✔   ✔   ✔

A. *From Capitularies Relating to the Army*[1]

779.

14. Let no one presume to gather an armed following (truste).

20. Let no one dare to sell any byrnies [coats-of-mail] outside of our realm.

803.

Ch. 7. Bucklers and byrnies shall not be given to the merchants.

801.

2. *De Haribanno.* If any free man, out of contempt for our command, shall have presumed to remain at home when the others go to war, let him know that he ought to

[1] From University of Pennsylvania, *Translations and Reprints,* VI, 5, pp. 6-7, 9, 10, 11.

pay the full *haribannum* according to the law of the Franks, that is, sixty solidi. Likewise, also, for contempt of single capitularies which we have promulgated by our royal authority, that is, any one who shall have broken the peace decreed for the churches of God, widows, orphans, wards, and the weak, shall pay the fine of sixty solidi.

3. Concerning deserters. If any one shall have shown himself so contumacious or haughty as to leave the army and return home without the command or permission of the king, that is, if he is guilty of what we call in the German language, *herisliz,* he himself, as a criminal, shall incur the peril of losing his life, and his property shall be confiscated for our treasury.

805.

6. Concerning the equipment in the army the same shall be observed as we have previously commanded in another capitulary, and, in particular, every man who possesses twelve mansi shall have a byrnie; he who has a byrnie and shall not have brought it with him shall lose his whole benefice, together with the byrnie.

7. Concerning the merchants who go to the countries of the Slavs and Avars, whither they ought to go on their business. . . . And they shall not carry arms and byrnies for sale; but if they shall have been discovered carrying any, all their property shall be taken from them; half shall go to the royal treasury, the other half shall be divided between the above mentioned *missi* and the discoverer.

19. Concerning the *haribannum* we will that our *missi* ought to exact it faithfully this year in accordance with our command, without indulgence for any person, either from favors or terror; that is, that they shall receive the lawful fine, namely three pounds, from each man who has six pounds in gold, silver, byrnies, brazen utensils, clothing, horses, oxen, cows, or other live stock; but the women and children shall not be deprived of their garments for this fine. Those who do not have the aforesaid property to the value of more than three pounds shall pay thirty solidi; etc. . . .

811.

3. If any man holding an office under us shall have been summoned to the host and shall not have come to the appointed muster, he shall abstain from flesh and wine for as many days as he shall have been proved to be late in coming to the appointed muster.

6. That in the host no one shall ask his peer or any other man to drink. And if any drunken person shall have been found in the army, he shall be so excommunicated that in drinking he shall use nothing but water until he acknowledges that he has acted wrongly.

8. It has been enacted that the preparation for serving in the army shall be defined and continued in accordance with the ancient custom, namely, victuals for a three months' march and arms and clothing for a half-year. But, nevertheless, it has been decided . . . that those who march from the Rhine to the Loire shall compute the beginning of their provision from the Loire, etc. . . .

10. It has been enacted that no bishop or abbot or abbess, or any rector or guardian of a church, shall presume without our permission to give or sell a byrnie or sword to any man outside, except only to his own vassals. And if it shall happen that he has in any church or sacred place more byrnies than are sufficient for the men who guard the same church, then the same rector of the church shall ask the king what ought to be done with these.

801-813.

10. That the equipments of the king shall be carried in carts, also the equipments of the bishops, counts, abbots, and nobles of the king; flour, wine, pork and victuals in abundance, mills, adzes, axes, augers, slings, and men who know how to use these well. And the marshals of the king shall add stones for these on twenty beasts of burden, if there is need. And each one shall be prepared for the army and shall have plenty of all utensils. And each count shall save two parts of the fodder in his county for the army's use, and he shall have good bridges, good boats.

B. *Letter of Charles to Abbot Fulrad,* 804-811: *Summons to the Army*[1]

In the name of the Father, Son and Holy Ghost. Charles, most serene, august, crowned by God, great pacific Emperor, and also, by God's mercy, King of the Franks and Lombards, to Abbot Fulrad.

Be it known to you that we have decided to hold our general assembly this year in the eastern part of Saxony, on the river Bode, at the place which is called Stassfurt. Therefore, we have commanded you to come to the aforesaid place, with all your men well armed and prepared, on the fifteenth day before the Kalends of July, that is, seven days before the festival of St. John the Baptist. Come, accordingly, so equipped with your men to the aforesaid place that thence you may be able to go well prepared in any direction whither our summons shall direct; that is, with arms and gear also, and other equipment for war in food and clothing. So that each horseman shall have a shield, lance, sword, dagger, bow and quivers with arrows; and in your carts utensils of various kinds, that is, axes, planes, augers, boards, spades, iron shovels, and other utensils which are necessary in an army. In the carts also supplies of food for three months, dating from the time of the assembly, arms and clothing for a half-year. And we command this in general, that you cause it to be observed that you proceed peacefully to the aforesaid place, through whatever part of our realm your journey shall take you, that is, that you presume to take nothing except fodder, wood and water; and let the men of each one of your vassals march along with the carts and horsemen, and let the leader always be with them until they reach the aforesaid place, so that the absence of a lord may not give an opportunity to his men of doing evil.

Send your gifts, which you ought to present to us at our assembly in the middle of the month of May, to the place where we then shall be; if perchance your journey shall so shape itself that on your march you are able in person to present these gifts of yours to us, we greatly desire it. See that you show no negligence in the future if you desire to have our favor.

[1] *Ibid.,* pp. 11-12.

c. *From Capitularies Relating to the Army: "Who Shall Go?"* [1]

807.

1. In the first place, all who seem to have benefices shall come to the army.

807 (?).

2. If it shall be necessary to furnish aid against the Saracens of Spain or the Avars, then five of the Saxons shall equip a sixth; and if it shall be necessary to bear aid against the Bohemians, two shall equip a third; if, indeed, there is need of defending the native country against the Sorbs, then all shall come together.

3. From the Frisians we will that the counts and our vassals, who seem to have benefices, and all the horsemen in general, shall come well prepared to our assembly; of the remaining poorer men six shall equip a seventh, and thus they shall come well prepared for war to the aforesaid assembly.

808.

1. Every free man who has four mansi of his own property, or as a benefice from any one, shall equip himself and go to the army, either with his lord, if the lord goes, or with his count. He who has three mansi, of his own property shall be joined to a man who has one mansus, and shall aid him so that he may serve for both. He who has only two mansi of his own property shall be joined to another who likewise has two mansi, and one of them, with the aid of the other, shall go to the army. He who has only one mansus of his own shall be joined to one of three who have the same and shall aid him, and the latter shall go alone; the three who have aided him shall remain at home.

4. From the men who have been enfeoffed by the counts the following are to be excepted and are not commanded to pay the ban: two who shall have been left behind with the wife of a count and two others who shall have been commanded to remain to guard his territory

[1] *Ibid.,* pp. 6, 8, 9.

and to perform our service. In this case we command, however, that each count shall leave at home two men to guard each separate territory which he has, in addition to those two who remain with his wife; all the others, without any exception, he shall have with him, or if he remains at home he shall order them to proceed with the one who goes to the army in his stead. A bishop or abbot shall leave at home two of those who are enfeoffed and laymen.

— Reading No. 12 —

IMPERIAL ADMINISTRATION

Among the difficult problems faced by Charlemagne's government was the question (as C. W. Previté-Orton formulated it) how to link "the administration of the local counts and immunist lords in his vast empire to the central government, a problem which began with the dissolution of the Roman State and continued to the end of the Middle Ages." Charles attempted to meet this problem with the new institution of the missi *and the analogous territorial division of the empire into* missatica: *to each of these two or three* missi *were sent each year with "the powers to inspect, redress and reform." The royal orders and instructions with which the* missi *were furnished dealt with all and sundry matters on all levels of government, including that of churches and abbeys in their districts. Top priority was given frequently to directives intended to protect the imperial dignity, authority, and property as well as those who had a special claim to the emperor's care and support.*

The General Capitulary for the Missi *of 802, excerpts of which are given below represents this type of royal order. It should be noted also that the* Capitula missorum *together with another type of capitularies, called* Capitula per se scribenda, *dealt with matters otherwise included in the* Capitularia ecclesiastica *and in the* Capitula legibus addenda (*supplement to the tribal codes*). *They, therefore, represent an interesting attempt of Charlemagne to supplement and to supersede local and specified laws on an empire-wide basis by the king's orders and by administrative procedure.*

✓   ✓   ✓

General Capitulary for the Missi, 802 [1]

FIRST CHAPTER. CONCERNING THE EMBASSY SENT OUT BY THE LORD EMPEROR. Therefore, the most serene and most Christian lord emperor Charles has chosen from his nobles the wisest and most prudent men, both archbishops and some of the other bishops also, and venerable abbots and pious laymen, and has sent them throughout his whole kingdom, and through them by all the following chapters has allowed men to live in accordance with the correct law. Moreover, where anything which is not right and just has been enacted in the law, he has ordered them to inquire into this most diligently and to inform him of it; he desired, God granting, to reform it. . . . And let the missi themselves make a diligent investigation whenever any man claims that an injustice has been done to him by any one, just as they desire to deserve the grace of omnipotent God and to keep their fidelity promised to Him, so that entirely in all cases everywhere, in accordance with the will and fear of God, they shall administer the law fully and justly in the case of the holy churches of God and of the poor, of wards and widows and of the whole people. And if there shall be anything of such a nature that they, together with the provincial counts, are not able of themselves to correct it and to do justice concerning it, they shall, without any ambiguity, refer this, together with their reports, to the judgment of the emperor; and the straight path of justice shall not be impeded by any one on account of flattery or gifts from any one,

[1] University of Pennsylvania, *Translations and Reprints,* VI, 5; excerpts from pp. 16-27.

or on account of any relationship, or from fear of the powerful.

2. Concerning the fidelity to be promised to the lord emperor. And he commanded that every man in his whole kingdom, whether ecclesiastic or layman, and each one according to his vow and occupation, should now promise to him as emperor the fidelity which he had previously promised to him as king; and all of those who had not yet made that promise should do likewise, down to those who were twelve years old. And that it shall be announced to all in public, so that each one might know, how great and how many things are comprehended in that oath; not merely as many have thought hitherto, fidelity to the lord emperor as regards his life, and not introducing any enemy into his kingdom out of enmity, and not consenting to or concealing another's faithlessness to him; but that all may know that this oath contains in itself this meaning.

4. Secondly, that no man, either through perjury or any other wile or fraud, on account of the flattery or gift of any one, shall refuse to give back or dare to abstract or conceal a serf of the lord emperor or a district or land or anything that belongs to him; and that no one shall presume, through perjury or other wile, to conceal or abstract his fugitive fiscaline serfs who unjustly and fraudulently say that they are free.

5. That no one shall presume to rob or do any injury fraudulently to the churches of God or widows or orphans or pilgrims; for the lord emperor himself, after God and His saints, has constituted himself their protector and defender.

6. That no one shall dare to lay waste a benefice of the lord emperor, or to make it his own property.

7. That no one shall presume to neglect a summons to war from the lord emperor; and that no one of the counts shall be so presumptuous as to dare to dismiss thence any one of those who owe military service, either on account of relationship or flattery or gifts from any one.

8. That no one shall presume to impede at all in any way a ban or command of the lord emperor, or to dally with his work or to impede or to lessen or in any way to act contrary to his will or commands. And that no one shall dare to neglect to pay his dues or tax.

10. That bishops and priests shall live according to the canons and shall teach others to do the same.

11. That bishops, abbots, abbesses, who are in charge of others with the greatest veneration shall strive to surpass their subjects in this diligence and shall not oppress their subjects with a harsh rule or tyranny, but with sincere love shall carefully guard the flock committed to them with mercy and charity or by the examples of good works.

12. That abbots shall live where the monks are and wholly with the monks, in accordance with the rule, and shall diligently learn and observe the canons; the abbesses shall do the same.

13. That bishops, abbots and abbesses shall have advocates, vicars and *centenarii*[1] who know the law and love justice, who are pacific and merciful, so that through these greater profit or advantage may accrue to the holy church of God; because we are entirely unwilling to have in the monasteries harmful and greedy provosts and advocates, from whom greater blasphemy or injury may arise for us. . . .

15. We will and command in every way that abbots and monks shall be subject to their bishops in all humility and obedience just as is commanded by the canonical constitution. . . .

16. Concerning choosing men for ordination, just as the lord emperor had formerly granted it, by the law of the Franks, to the bishops and abbots, so he has also now confirmed it; nevertheless, in this manner, so that neither a bishop nor an abbot in a monastery shall prefer the more worthless to the better. . . .

17. Moreover, that the monks shall live firmly and strictly in accordance with the rule, because we know that any one whose goodwill is lukewarm is displeasing to God, as John bears witness in the Apocalypse:[2] "I would that thou wert cold or hot. So then, because thou art lukewarm and neither cold nor hot, I will spue thee out of my mouth." Let them in no way usurp to themselves secular business. . . .

[1] A *centenarius* is the official of a *centena;* the latter is a subdivision of a province or county.
[2] Rev., iii. 15, 16.

18. Monasteries for women shall be firmly ruled, and the women shall not be permitted to wander about at all, but they shall be guarded with all diligence, and they shall not presume to arouse litigations or strife among themselves, nor shall they dare to be disobedient or refractory in any way toward their superiors and abbesses. . . .

22. Moreover, the canonical clergy shall observe fully the canonical life, and shall be instructed at the episcopal residence or in the monastery with all diligence according to the canonical discipline. They shall not be permitted to wander outside at all, but shall live under strict guardianship, not given to base gain, not fornicators, not thieves, not homicides, not robbers, not quarrelsome, not wrathful, not proud, not drunken, but with a chaste heart and body, humble, modest, sober, merciful, pacific, that as sons of God they may be worthy to be promoted in the sacred order; not in the villages or villas near to or adjoining the churches, without a master and without discipline, like those who are called sarabaites, living in luxury or fornication or other iniquity, to consent to which is absurd.

24. If, moreover, any priest or deacon shall presume hereafter to have with him in his house any women except those whom the canonical license permits, he shall be deprived of both his office and inheritance until he be brought to our presence.

26. That judges shall judge justly in accordance with the written law, and not according to their own will.

27. And we command that no one in our whole kingdom shall dare to deny hospitality to rich or poor or pilgrims, that is, no one shall deny shelter and fire and water to pilgrims traversing our country in God's name, or to anyone travelling for the love of God or for the safety of his own soul. If, moreover, any one shall wish to serve them farther, let him expect the best reward from God, who Himself said: "And whoso shall receive one such little child in my name, receiveth me;" [1] and elsewhere: "I was a stranger and ye took me in." [2]

28. Concerning embassies coming from the lord emperor. That the counts and centenarii shall provide most

[1] Matthew, xviii. 5.   [2] Matthew, xxv. 35.

carefully, as they desire the grace of the lord emperor, for the missi who are sent out, so that they may go through their departments without any delay. . . .

30. Concerning those whom the lord emperor wishes, Christ being propitious, to enjoy peace and protection in his kingdom, namely, those who are hastening to his clemency, either Christians or pagans, because they desire to announce some news, or seeking his aid on account of their poverty or hunger, that no one shall dare to constrain them to serve him, or to seize them, or alienate or sell them. . . .

32. Murders, by which a multitude of the Christian people perishes, we command in every way to be shunned and to be forbidden; God Himself forbade to His followers hatred and enmity, much more murder. . . . When by the persuasions of the devil murders happen, the criminal shall immediately hasten to make amends and with all celerity shall pay the fitting composition for the evil done to the relatives of the murdered man. And we forbid firmly, that the relatives of the murdered man shall dare in any way to continue their enmities on account of the evil done, or shall refuse to grant peace to him who asks it, but having given their pledges they shall receive the fitting composition and shall make a perpetual peace; moreover, the guilty one shall not delay to pay the composition. . . .

33. We prohibit in every way the crime of incest. . . .

35. That all shall wholly venerate their bishops and priests with all honor in the service and will of God. That they shall not dare to pollute themselves and others by incestuous nuptials; that they shall not presume to be married before the bishops and priests together with the elders of the people have inquired diligently into the consanguinity of those marrying; and then they shall be married with a benediction. . . .

36. . . . If any one after this shall have been proved a perjurer, let him know that he shall lose his right hand; and they shall be deprived of their property until we shall render our decision.

39. That in our forests no one shall dare to steal our game, which we have already many times forbidden to be done. . . .

40. Lastly, therefore, we desire all our decrees to be known in our whole kingdom through our missi now sent out, either among the men of the church, bishops, abbots, priests, deacons, canons, all monks or nuns. . . . Likewise also to the laymen and in all places everywhere.

— Reading No. 13 —

SOCIAL CHANGES

The documents contained in this Reading are selected to illustrate the institutions and social changes that paved the way for the characteristic class conditions and relationships of the feudal society in the earlier Middle Ages. Among the old Roman-Frankish institutions now adapted to the needs of a growing state and society such as bene-fice, precaria, *immunity,* commendatio, *the two latter are exemplified by 13A and 13B. Formulae of this type for all of the four mentioned institutions were in use throughout the Frankish era. The Carolingians must have found in these institutions much that was useful for the strengthening of the coherency and military efficiency of the Frankish army. They gave them legal sanction in regulations such as those inserted in the Capitulary of Mersen, 847 (13C). The general conditions worked in favor of a privileged and wealthy landowning class which monopolized all the political rights and duties while "the poor" lost, along with their land, their legal status as freemen as well as freedom of movement.*

Documents 13D, 13E, and 13F show Charlemagne's concern with the deterioration of the poorer freemen and the remedies which he tried to apply to cure these ills. For his policy of lessening the burden of military service for the poor freeman by introducing a quota system; see the excerpts from the Capitularies of 807 and 808 in Reading 11C.

✓   ✓   ✓

A. *A Grant of Immunity (Seventh Century)*[1]

Therefore, may your greatness or perseverance know that we have seen fit to concede by our ready will to such and such an illustrious man, the vill named so and so, situated in such and such a district, completely with its whole proper boundary, as it has been possessed by such and such a one or by our treasury, or is possessed at this present time. Wherefore, by our present authority we have decreed what we command shall be kept forever that the man aforesaid, so and so, should have conceded to him, such and such a vill we have said, in its entirety, with the lands, houses, buildings, villeins, slaves, vineyards, woods, fields, meadows, pastures etc. in entire immunity, and without the entrance of any one of the judges for the purpose of holding the pleas of any kind of causes. Thus he may have, hold, and possess it in proprietary right and without expecting the entrance of any one of the judges; and may leave the possession of it to his posterity, by the aid of God from our bounty, or to whom he will; and by our permission he shall have free power to do whatever he may wish with it for the future. And in order that this authority may be held as more firm, we have decreed it to be corroborated below with our own hand.

B. *A Formula of Commendation (Seventh Century)*[2]

To that magnificent lord *so and so,* I, *so and so:* Since it is known familiarly to all how little I have whence to feed and clothe myself, I have therefore petitioned your piety, and your goodwill has decreed to me that I should hand myself over or commend myself to your guardianship, which I have thereupon done; that is to say in this way, that you should aid and succor me as well with food as with clothing, according as I shall be able to serve

---

[1] From N. Downs, *Basic Documents in Medieval History* (Princeton, Van Nostrand, 1959), no. 18, pp. 44-45.
[2] *Ibid.,* no. 19, pp. 45-46.

you and deserve it.

And so long as I shall live I ought to provide service and honor to you, suitably to my free condition; and I shall not during the time of my life have the ability to withdraw from your power or guardianship; but must remain during the days of my life under your power or defence. Wherefore it is proper that if either of us shall wish to withdraw himself from these agreements, he shall pay *so many* shillings to his peer and this agreement shall remain unbroken. . . .

c. *The Capitulary of Mersen, 847* [1]

We will moreover that each free man in our kingdom shall choose a lord, from us or our faithful, such a one as he wishes.

We command moreover that no man shall leave his lord without just cause, nor should any one receive him, except in such a way as was customary in the time of our predecessors.

And we wish you to know that we want to grant right to our faithful subjects and we do not wish to do anything to them against reason. Similarly we admonish you and the rest of our faithful subjects that you grant right to your men and do not act against reason toward them.

And we will that the man of each one of us [Lothair, Louis, and Charles] in whosesoever kingdom he is, shall go with his lord against the enemy, or in his other needs unless there shall have been (as may there not be) such an invasion of the kingdom as is called a *landwer,* so that the whole people of that kingdom shall go together to repel it.

d. *From the Capitulary Issued in Thionville* (Theodonis Villa) for the *Missi (Date?)* [2]

4. In case of famine, devastation, pestilence, tempest or other such tribulation no edict of ours should be waited for, but God's mercy should be invoked without delay. As regards this year's famine, let everybody succor his

[1] *Ibid.,* no. 20, pp. 46-47.
[2] Translated by H. W. from *Capitularia regum Francorum* I (*Mon. Germ. Hist., Legum sectio* II, 1), no. 44, pp. 122-123.

people [tenants] as well as he can and let him not sell his grain too high and not sell any foodstuff outside the empire.

15. Freemen who want to devote themselves to the service of God should ask for our permission before they do so. We learned that some of them do this not out of devotion but to escape military service or other royal services; others feel that they are threatened by the greed of those who covet their property. We altogether forbid this.

16. Concerning the oppression of poor freemen: they should not be oppressed by magnates who deal unjustly and ill-intentionedly with them so that under pressure they sell or surrender their estates to them. We give this order here and above [15] concerning the freemen so that their relatives should not be unlawfully disinherited, the king's service diminished, and heirs forced by want to become robbers and criminals. . . .

E. *Canons from the Council of Tours*, 813 [1]

44. For various reasons the property of the poor has considerably diminished in many places, that is, the property of those who are known as freemen but who are now under the power of magnates. If our most pious and gracious prince would order a diligent investigation into these conditions and their causes, many would be found who for various reasons have been reduced to extreme poverty.

49. The lords should be admonished to deal with their subjects in a charitable and merciful way; they should neither oppress them nor take away their property unlawfully, nor should their debts be collected in a ruthless and cruel manner.

F. *Capitulary Concerning Matters to be Discussed with Bishops and Abbots*, 811 [2]

5. Inquiry should be made about those who have left this world but who are trying daily to increase their pos-

[1] Translated by H. W. from *Concilia aevi Karolini* I, (*Mon. Germ. Hist., Legum sectio* III, 2), pp. 292-293.

[2] Translated by H. W. from *Capitularia regum Francorum* I (*Mon. Germ. Hist., Legum sectio* II, 1), no. 72, p. 163.

sessions in every way by promising the bliss of the heavenly kingdom or threatening eternal punishment. In the name of God they deprive of their possession the rich as well as the poor, those, that is, who are simple-minded and uneducated; they also rob their legitimate heirs of their inheritance. Hence they force these people to commit shameful actions and crimes because of their poverty. . . .

— Reading No. 14 —

REFORM OF THE FRANKISH CHURCH

The reform of the Frankish Church was in the main the work of the Anglo-Saxon priest and monk Winfrid-Boniface, though it was supported by the prestige and the authority of the popes and executed by the politics of the Frankish mayors of the palace. As his main source of inspiration Boniface drew on the religious and scholarly education and the tradition in which he was raised in Anglo-Saxon England. Time and again he turned to his Anglo-Saxon friends and relatives, princes, priests, monks and nuns for material help and spiritual comfort (14A, 14B). Boniface maintained a lively correspondence not only with his friends across the channel but also with the popes and the Frankish princes and bishops. From this correspondence, which is a mine of information for historians, since important documents other than letters are inserted, most of the documents included in this Reading are taken. The following documents are selected to illustrate important phases and aspects of the Reform: the oath taken by Boniface to Pope Gregory II (14C); excerpts from letters by Pope Gregory II and Pope Zacharias written in answer to questions of Boniface concerning matters of morality and the policy to be followed in cases of irregular or disorderly ceremonies such as baptism and consecration, of immoral and renegade priests, and the like (14D); a letter of Pope Gregory II confirming the new organization introduced by Boniface for Bavaria (14E). The help and the advice of the popes were important: as successors to Saint Peter they enjoyed an ever-increasing prestige and authority. But Boniface himself admitted that he would have achieved little without the ecclesiastical policy of the Carolingians, which was, in general, favorable to Boniface's program of reform.

Excerpts from the decrees published by Carloman at the Synods of the Austrasian Church in 742 and in Lestinnes in 743 (14F) show that the Carolingians were concerned with the issues of the Church. Besides, Carloman was intent, as was his brother Pepin at the Synod of Soissons, 744, to eliminate the controversy with the Church concerning the lands confiscated by Charles Martel, their father, for the equipment of warriors with benefices. Since Carloman's promise of 742 to make full restitution of all Church property according to the request of the clergy could not be realized without great harm to the military defence of the kingdom, new arrangements were made at the Synod of Lestinnes. These were later replaced by those of Charlemagne at the Synod of Heristal, 779 (14H). The preamble and the first five paragraphs of Pepin's Capitulary containing the decisions of his reform synod held 755 at Ver are representative of his effort to continue Boniface's reform but to withhold decision on solutions that might meet with resistance on the side of the Frankish clergy (14G).

✓   ✓   ✓

A. *Boniface Calls upon All Anglo-Saxons to Pray for the Conversion of the Saxons, c 738* [1]

To all his reverend fellow bishops . . . and, in general, to all God-fearing Catholics of the stock and race of the Angles, Boniface named also Winfred, born of that same

[1] From *The Letters of Saint Boniface,* translated by E. Emerton (New York, 1940), no. XXXVI, pp. 74-75.

race, German legate of the Church Universal, servant of
the Apostolic See and called Archbishop for no merit of
his own, sends greetings of humble communion and un-
feigned love in Christ.

We earnestly beseech your brotherly goodness to be
mindful of us, who are worth so little, in your prayers
that we may be delivered from the snare of Satan, the
huntsman, and from wicked and cruel men, that the word
of God may make its way and be glorified. We beseech
you to obtain through your holy prayers, that our Lord
and God Jesus Christ, "who will have all men to be saved,
and to come unto the knowledge of God," may turn the
hearts of the pagan Saxons to the Catholic faith, that
they may free themselves from the snares of the devil in
which they are bound and may be gathered among the
children of the Mother Church.

Take pity upon them; for they themselves are saying:
"We are of one blood and one bone with you." . . .

B. *Boniface Asks the Abbess Eadburga to Make Him
a Copy of the Epistles of St. Peter in Letters of Gold,
735* [1]

To his most reverend and beloved sister, the abbess
Eadburga, Boniface, humble servant of the servants of
God, sends heartfelt greetings of love in Christ.

I pray to Almighty God, the rewarder of all good
works, that He will repay you in the heavenly mansions
and eternal tabernacles and in the choir of the blessed
angels for all the kindnesses you have shown me, the
solace of books and the comfort of the garments with
which you have relieved my distress.

And I beg you further to add to what you have done
already by making a copy written in gold of the Epistles
of my master, St. Peter the Apostle, to impress honor and
reverence for the Sacred Scriptures visibly upon the car-
nally minded to whom I preach. I desire to have ever
present before me the words of him who is my guide upon
this road. I am sending by the priest Eoban the materials
for your writing.

[1] *Ibid.*, no. XXVI, pp. 64-65.

Do then, dearest sister, with this petition of mine as you have always done with my requests, so that here also your works may shine forth in gold letters for the glory of our heavenly Father. I pray for your well-being in Christ, and may you go upward to still greater heights of holy virtue.

c. The Oath of Bishop Boniface, November 30, 722 [1]

In the name of the Lord God and of our Savior, Jesus Christ. In the sixth year of Leo, by the grace of God emperor, in the sixth year of his consulship and in the fourth year of his son, the Emperor Constantine, in the sixth indiction:

I, Boniface, by the grace of God bishop, promise you, O blessed Peter, chief of the Apostles, and to your vicar, the blessed Pope Gregory and to his successors, in the name of the Father, the Son, and the Holy Spirit, the indivisible Trinity, and of this, thy most sacred body, that I will show entire faith and sincerity toward the holy Catholic doctrine and will persist in the unity of the same, so God help me—that faith in which, beyond a doubt, the whole salvation of Christians consists. I will in no wise agree to anything which is opposed to the unity of the Church Universal, no matter who shall try to persuade me; but I will, as I have said, show in all things a perfect loyalty to you and to the welfare of your Church, to which the power to bind and loose is given by God, and to your vicar and his successors.

But, if I shall discover any bishops who are opponents of the ancient institutions of the holy Fathers, I will have no part nor lot with them, but so far as I can will restrain them or, if that is impossible, will make a true report to my apostolic master. But if (which God forbid!) I should be tempted into any action contrary to this my promise in any way or by any device or pretext whatsoever, may I be found guilty at the last judgment and suffer the punishment of Ananias and Sapphira, who dared to defraud you by making a false declaration of their property.

[1] *Ibid.*, no. VIII, p. 41.

D. *Papal Replies to Questions of Boniface*[1]

1. GREGORY II, 726.

You ask first within what degrees of relationship marriage may take place. We reply, strictly speaking, in so far as the parties know themselves to be related they ought not to be joined together. But since moderation is better than strictness of discipline especially toward so uncivilized a people, they may contract marriage after the fourth degree.

As to your question what a man is to do if his wife is unable, on account of disease, to fulfil her wifely duty: it would be well if he could remain in a state of continence. But since this is a matter of great difficulty it is better for him who cannot refrain to take a wife. He may not, however, withdraw his support from the one who was prevented by disease, provided she be not involved in any grievous fault. . . .

As to young children taken from their parents and not knowing whether they have been baptized or not, reason requires you to baptize them, unless there be someone who can give evidence in the case.

Lepers if they are believing Christians, may receive the body and blood of the Lord, but they may not take food together with persons in health.

You ask whether in the case of contagious disease or plague in a church or monastery, those who are not yet attacked may escape danger by flight. We declare this to be the height of folly: for no one can escape from the hand of God. . . .

2. POPE ZACHARIAS, 748

You report also, my brother, that you have found so-called priests,[2] more in number than the true Catholics,

---

[1] *Ibid.*, nos. XVIII, LXIV, digested from pp. 53-55, 142-145.
[2] This description does not, of course, refer to the clergy in the old Frankish lands but to priests in the new missionary districts, who of necessity had often to be chosen from among the newly converted Christians whose faith and actions were still far from conformity with Roman Christianity.

heretical pretenders under the name of bishops or priests but never ordained by Catholic bishops. They lead the people astray and bring confusion into the service of the Church. Some are false vagrants, adulterers, murderers, effeminates, pederasts, blasphemers, hypocrites, and many of them are tonsured serfs who have fled from their masters, servants of the devil transformed into ministers of Christ, who, subject to no bishop, live according to their own caprice, protected by the people against the bishops, so that these have no check upon their scandalous conduct. They gather about them a like-minded following and carry on their false ministry, not in a Catholic church, but in the open country in the huts of farm laborers, where their ignorance and stupid folly can be hidden from the bishops. They neither preach the Catholic faith to pagans, nor have they themselves the true faith. They do not even know the sacred words any catechumen old enough to use his reason can learn and understand, nor do they expect them to be uttered by those whom they are to baptize, as, for instance, the renunciation of Satan, and so forth. Neither do they fortify them with the sign of the cross, which should precede baptism, nor do they teach them belief in one God and the Holy Trinity; nor do they require them to believe with the heart for righteousness or to make confession with the lips for salvation.

Wherever, beloved, you find these ministers, not of Christ but of Satan, you will call a meeting of the clergy of the province and utterly reject them. You will strip them of their priestly functions and order them to spend their lives in penance under monastic rule. Thus disciplined in the body, if they ever turn to the right way and believe in their hearts, let a true confession with the lips witness to their salvation. But even if they shall not be converted, the justice of your decision shall not be denied. For you will have as your consolation against the iniquity of evildoers the canonical sanction of the holy Apostles and other recognized fathers.

E. *Pope Gregory III to Boniface. Organization of the Church in Bavaria,* October 29, 739 [1]

Gregory, servant of the servants of God, to Boniface, his reverend and holy brother and fellow bishop.

The teacher of all nations, the eminent Apostle Paul spoke, saying: "All things work together for good to them that love God." When we learned from your report that God in His mercy had deigned to set free so many in Germany from the power of the heathen and had brought as many as a hundred thousand souls into the bosom of Mother Church through your efforts and those of Charles, prince of the Franks, and when we heard what you had accomplished in Bavaria, we lifted up our hands to heaven in thanks to the Lord our God, giver of all good, who opened the gates of mercy and loving-kindness in those western lands for the knowledge of the way of salvation and sent his angel to prepare the way before you. Glory be to Him forever and ever!

You inform us that you have visited the Bavarian people and found that they were not living in accordance with the prescriptions of the Church, that there was but one bishop in that province, a certain Uiuilo [Wilhelm?] whom we ordained a long time ago, and that you have, with the approval of Odilo, duke of those same Bavarians, and of the nobles of that province, ordained three other bishops. You have also divided the province into four districts, so that each bishop may have his own diocese. In all this you have acted well and wisely, my brother, since you have fulfilled the apostolic precepts in our stead and have done as we directed you. Cease not therefore, most reverend brother, to teach them the holy Catholic and apostolic tradition of the Roman See, that the natives may be enlightened and may follow in the way of salvation and so may gain eternal reward.

As to the priests whom you have found there: if those who ordained them are unknown and it is uncertain whether they were bishops or not, if the priests are Catholic men and of good repute, trained in the service of Christ, well versed in the whole sacred law, and fitted for their office, then let each receive from his bishop the

[1] *Ibid.,* no. XXXV, pp. 72-73.

priestly benediction and consecration and so perform the duties of his sacred office.

It is advisable that those who were baptized according to the varieties and the inflections of the heathen dialects, provided they were baptized in the name of the Trinity, should be confirmed with the sacred chrism and the laying on of hands. . . .

In regard to a council which you are to hold in the Danube valley in our stead: we direct Your Fraternity to be present there vested with apostolic authority. In so far as God shall give you strength, cease not to preach the Word of Salvation that the faith of Christ may increase and multiply in the name of God.

You are not at liberty, my brother, to linger in one place when your work there is done; but strengthen the hearts of the brethren and of all the faithful throughout those regions of the West, and wherever God shall open to you a way to save souls, carry on your preaching. . . .

F. *From the Decrees of the Synods of 742 and 743 Published by Carloman, Palace Mayor of the Eastern Franks*[1]

742.

In the name of our Lord Jesus Christ, I, Carloman, duke and prince of the Franks, in the seven hundred and forty-second year of the Incarnation of Christ and the twenty-first day of April, by the advice of the servants of God and my chief men, have brought together in the fear of Christ the bishops of my realm with their priests into a council or synod; namely, Archbishop Boniface, Burchard [of Würzburg], Reginfried [of Cologne], etc. . . .

And by the advice of my priests and nobles we have appointed bishops for the several cities and have set over them as archbishop Boniface, the delegate of St. Peter.

We have ordered that a synod shall be held every year, so that in our presence the canonical decrees and the laws of the Church may be reëstablished and the Christian religion purified. Revenues, of which churches were

[1] From *The Letters of Boniface, loc. cit.*, no. XLIV, pp. 91-99.

defrauded, we have restored and given back to them. We have deprived false priests and adulterous or lustful deacons of their church incomes, have degraded them, and forced them to do penance.

We have absolutely forbidden the servants of God to carry arms or fight, to enter the army or march against an enemy, except only so many as are especially selected for divine service such as celebrating Mass or carrying relics—that is to say: the prince may have one or two bishops with the chaplains, and each praefect one priest to hear confessions and prescribe penance. We have also forbidden the servants of God to hunt or wander about the woods with dogs or to keep hawks and falcons.

We have also ordered, according to the sacred canons, that every priest living within a diocese shall be subject to the bishop of that diocese. Annually during Lent he shall render to that bishop an account of his ministry. . . .

We have decreed, according to the canons, that every bishop within his own diocese and with the help of the count, who is the defender of the Church, shall see to it that the people of God perform no pagan rites but reject and cast out all the foulness of the heathen, such as sacrifices to the dead, casting of lots, divinations, amulets and auguries, incantations, or offering of animals, which foolish folk perform in the churches, according to pagan custom, in the name of holy martyrs or confessors, thereby calling down the wrath of God and his saints and also those sacrilegious fires which they call "Niedfeor," and whatever other pagan practices there may be. . . .

We have decreed also that priests and deacons shall not wear cloaks after the fashion of laymen, but cassocks according to the usage of the servants of God. . . .

743.

. . . The whole body of the clergy—bishops, priests, deacons, and clerks—accepting the canons of the ancient fathers, have promised to restore the laws of the Church as to morals and doctrine and form of service. Abbots and monks have accepted the Rule of the holy father, Benedict, for the reformation of the regular life. . . .

We order also, by the advice of the servants of God and of the Christian people and in view of imminent wars and attacks by the foreign populations which surround us, that a portion of the properties of the Church shall be used for some time longer, with God's indulgence, for the benefit of our army, as a *precarium* and paying a *census,* on condition, however, that annually from each *casata* [of these ecclesiastical estates] one *solidus,* that is twelve *denarii,* shall be paid to the church or monastery which owns it. In case of the death of the persons to whom the property was entrusted as a *precarium,* it shall revert to the Church. Also, if conditions are such that the prince deems it necessary, let the *precarium* be renewed for another term and a new contract be written. But let extreme care be taken that churches and monasteries whose property is granted in *precarium* shall not be reduced to poverty and suffer want; and, if they should thus be distressed, let the whole property be given back to the church and the house of God.

G. *From the Capitulary Issued at the Reform Synod under Pepin,* 755 [1]

The ancient rules of the fathers, if they had remained intact, would have been sufficient to correct the evildoers. But emergencies, misfortunes, and unruly times have arisen and several of these rules have been allowed to lapse. Therefore, the most glorious and pious Pepin, illustrious king of the Franks, convened all the bishops of Gaul at Ver [lower Seine] in his palace for the sake of restoring some of these rules. Since means are lacking to restore them in their entirety, at least he wishes to correct the abuses that are most harmful to the welfare of the Church. If more serene times and a quiet interim be granted to him by Heaven later on, he intends to implement the rules in their entirety. . . . For the moment and under the pressure of necessity some of them must be omitted. . . . In the meantime, to the best of our

[1] Translated by H. W. from *Capitularia regum Francorum* I, no. 14 (*Mon. Germ. Hist., Legum sectio* II, 1), pp. 33-34.

abilities, let us try to keep them unharmed and untouched. . . .

[It was decided:]

1. that there should be bishops in every single *civitas;*
2. that the bishops whom we establish as substitutes for
   metropolitans should be obeyed by the other bishops
   until the time when we restore them fully according to
   canonical institutions;
3. that every bishop use his authority in his diocese (*parrochia*) to correct the clergy, both regular and secular,
   and urge them to mend their ways according to their
   spiritual and canonical rules so that they may live a
   God-pleasing life;
4. that there be a synod each year . . . and that
   especially all those bishops should attend whom we
   established in the place of archbishops and all such
   bishops, abbots, and priests whom these metropolitans
   order to appear . . . ;
5. that monasteries, whether of men or virgins (*puellae*),
   should live according to their rule and if they fail to
   do so the bishop in his diocese should correct them.
   . . . If the bishop cannot correct them they should
   appear before the synod and receive a canonical sentence. And if the bishop holds the synod in contempt
   he will either lose his honor or be excommunicated
   by all the bishops, and by the order and the will of the
   king, and with the consent of the servants of God another bishop will be put in his place who rules his
   flock according to the holy regulations.

H. *From the Capitulary of Heristal,* 779 [1]

13. From church land for which a rent (*census*) is
now paid, a tenth and a ninth should be given in addition to the rent; and from those church lands for which
hitherto no rents have been paid there should now be
given a ninth and a tenth, and a shilling for fifty houses,
half a shilling for thirty houses, and a third for twenty

[1] From *Capitularia regum Francorum* I, no. 20 (*Mon. Germ.
Hist., Legum sectio* II, 1), p. 50. Adapted from a transla-
tion of the passage by G. Constable, "Nona et Decima,"
Speculum, XXXV (1960), p. 226.

houses. Old *precaria* should be renewed; but where there are none, they should be written down. And *precaria* made at our order [*verbo regis*] should be distinguished from *precaria* made from the lands of churches by their own free will.

— Reading No. 15 —

CHARLES AS A THEOLOGIAN

The Synod of Frankfurt, assembled in 794 and attended by the Frankish clergy and also by two representatives of Pope Hadrian I and a few delegates of the Anglo-Saxon Church, demonstrates in a spectacular way the role assumed by Charles in the Christian Church as the supreme authority in all matters, including doctrine and faith. Charles himself presided over the assembly, gave direction as to its agenda, opened it with a "keynote speech" and attended the sessions not only as a witness—auditor—but as the one who made and announced the final decisions—arbiter (15D and 15C). The Libri Carolini, *though composed by his scholars (Alcuin), represented his own views on the question of image worship, and it is for good reasons that this bulky work was named for him. From the* Libri Carolini, *issued as* Capitulare de imaginibus, *we give two short excerpts: the first reveals Charles's criticism of the high-handed manner in which the Church of Constantinople had superimposed its decisions on all the other churches without consulting them and his unwillingness to accept Byzantine leadership in any matters whatsoever. The second contains the formula-*

tion of the doctrine of image worship as conceived by Charles and his theologians (15A and 15B).

✓ ✓ ✓

A. From the Libri Carolini *on the Claim of the "Council" of Nicaea to be Ecumenical* [1]

To the claim [to be universal] the actions of the Church [of Constantinople] form a marked contrast. For it attempted in a presumptuous and imprudent manner to excommunicate all the Churches of the world before it had consulted them by letters and in accordance with ecclesiastical customs had asked for their opinion. It should have made an inquiry by delegates in all the Churches of the adjacent provinces as to whether or not they wished to adore images. In this way . . . the church of Constantinople itself would have been bound to accept the decision of the majority of the Churches according to apostolic regulations, and to condemn to abomination the Church that would have attempted to oppose the institutions of old against the consent of the majority and to break away from the universal body of the Church.

B. From the Libri Carolini: *Formulation of the Frankish Doctrine of Image Worship* [2]

God alone we should worship, adore and glorify. Of Him alone the Prophet said that his name was exalted. We also owe veneration to His saints who defeated the devil and who are now reigning with Him. Bravely they fought, to transmit to us unharmed the state of the Church or, as we know, assisted the Church constantly with their contributions and interventions. The worshiping and adoration of images, however, should be entirely abolished. The question whether or not the images were installed in memory of deeds or for decoration [of Churches] does not affect in any way the Catholic faith itself since images have hardly any function in the performance of the mystery that involves our salvation.

[1] Translated by H. W. from the *Libri Carolini ed.* H. Bastgen (*Mon. Germ. Hist., Legum sectio* III, *Concilia* II, *Supplementum*), III, 11, p. 123.
[2] *Ibid.,* II, 21, p. 80.

C. *From the Capitulary Issued by King Charles at Frankfurt on the Iconoclastic Question*[1]

2. The question [of image worship] which had been decided at the new Greek synod [Nicaea, 787], that is the one that dealt with the adoration of images and was later transferred to Constantinople, was also discussed at the Synod [of Frankfurt]. In it [the Decree of Nicaea-Constantinople] the point had been made that those who did not worship or adore the images of the saints in the way they adored and worshipped the Divine Trinity would be excommunicated. But our holy fathers altogether refused contemptuously the adoration of and the obsequy to images and condemned those who consented to it.

D. *From a Statement Made by the Italian Bishops at the Synod of Frankfurt on the Question of Adoptionism*[2]

. . . On a certain day when all were assembled in the hall of the sacred palace and the priests, deacons and the rest of the clergy were standing round the king the letter of Eliphand, archbishop of Toledo (near the province of Seville), was brought to the presence of the king. At his order it was read out in public. Then, the venerable prince arose from his throne and, standing on the dais, addressed the assembly with a long sermon on the matter of faith (*de causa fidei*) adding the following: "What is your opinion? Ever since last year . . . this abominable error has increased in this region, nay, has spread to the farthest corners of our kingdom. We must necessarily stamp it out by all possible means with the help of ecclesiastical censure." . . .

[1] Translated by H.W. from *Capitularia regum Francorum* I (*Mon. Germ. Hist., Legum sectio* II, 1), no. 28, pp. 73-74.

[2] Translated by H.W. from the *Libellus episcoporum Italiae*, *Concilia aevi Karolini* I (*Mon. Germ. Hist., Legum sectio* III, 2), p. 131.

— Reading No. 16 —

POLITICAL THEORY

In the face of the ever-increasing pressure of the emperors in the East to superimpose their doctrinal decisions on the Roman Church, popes of the fifth century felt the necessity to strike at the heart of the problem of the relations between pope and emperor. To the claim that the emperor was rex and sacerdos, king and priest, like David or even like Christ, Pope Leo I answered by restating the Petrine doctrine and by emphasizing the spiritual apostolate of the successors to St. Peter: "Your city is royal but you cannot make it apostolic" he told the emperor of "New-Rome."

Further clarification as to the nature and the relationship of the two powers was attempted by Pope Gelasius I (492-496) in his treatises and letters, the most famous of which, Duo quippe sunt, is included here (16A). Drawing a line between the two and defining their nature as auctoritas and potestas respectively he implies that the spiritual power is the higher, that is, in the language of the time, sacred, while the temporal owns only the power to execute what the former laid down as binding (W. Ullman). He further elaborates on this point by stating that the burden (pondus) of the priesthood is all the "heavier" as it deals with salvation. But, on the other hand, Gelasius wants each order to perform its separate and divinely instituted function without interference of the one into the sphere of the other. Charlemagne was, no doubt, imbued with this ideology by his clerical advisers and teachers. But he was inclined to draw the line between the two powers differently. To be sure, the purity and orthodoxy of the Christian Church and faith was his foremost preoccupation and he was convinced that this goal could only be reached by close collaboration with the Roman pontiff. But how small a role he assigned to the pope in its achievement can best be seen from a famous letter written by King Charles to Pope Leo III four years be-

166

*fore his coronation (16B). In matters of doctrine Charles
assigned to the pope what has been called a magisterial
or doctrinal primacy, while for himself he assumed all
jurisdictional primacy.*

*After Charles's death a reaction set in: the Frankish
clergy resented royal interference in spiritual and ecclesiastical matters just as much as the popes of the fifth
century had disliked the caesaropapism of the eastern
emperors. Hence, the attempt to restore the balance. Theoretically, this was done at several Frankish synods by
the new formulation of the Gelasian theory. Much later
—in the age of the Gregorian reform—the Gelasian statement which in the mind of many a medieval thinker contained the ideal guaranty for the maintenance of peace
and order in the Christian society, was clad in the more
colorful biblical metaphor of the two swords (Luke xxii.
38). We bring it here (16C) in the formulation of the
great reformer Petrus Damiani. It may serve as an example of the persistency of medieval tradition, which in
spite of distortions and misinterpretations, Carolingian
and otherwise, was still very much alive as late as the
age of Dante (16D).*

✓   ✓   ✓

A. *From a Letter of Pope Gelasius I to Emperor Anastasius,* 494 [1]

There are, august Emperor, two [powers] which essentially rule the world: the sacred authority (*auctoritas*)
of the pontiffs and the royal power (*potestas*). But the
burden of the priests is the heavier one since they will
have to render account even over the rulers of men at
the divine tribunal. For you know, dearest son, that
although you are first in dignity among the human race
you bend your head humbly before the ministers of the
things divine expecting assistance for the salvation of
your soul and knowing that you submit to, rather than
control, the religious rites of the holy sacraments and
their dispensation. Therefore in these matters you de-

[1] Translated by H. W. from K. Mirbt, *Quellen zur Geschichte
des Papsttums und des Römischen Katholizismus,* 5. Auf-
lage (Tübingen, 1934), no. 187, p. 85.

pend on their judgment and you cannot make them subject to your will. The priests of your religion, on the other hand, are willing to obey your laws as they refer to public order; for they know that secular jurisdiction has been conferred upon you from above; therefore they would not oppose your decisions in matters concerning this world. Should not you then with even greater devotion obey those who dispense the venerable mysteries that are so much in demand?

B. *King Charles to Pope Leo on the Two Powers*, 796 [1] (*cf. Reading No. 8*B).

As I have done with your predecessor . . . I desire to establish with your blessedness an inviolable covenant of faith and charity so that divine mercy obtained by the prayers of your apostolic holiness and your apostolic blessing may follow me everywhere while, God willing, the most holy see of the Roman Church will always be defended by our devotion. Indeed it is our task with divine help to shield everywhere with our arms the Holy Church of Christ from all her enemies abroad, from the incursions of the heathen and the devastations of the infidel, and to fortify her from within by the profession of the Catholic faith. It is your task, Holy Father, to assist the success of our arms with your hands raised in prayer to God like Moses so that by your intervention, God willing and granting, the Christian people will for ever achieve victory over the enemies of His name, and the name of our Lord Jesus Christ will be glorified throughout the world.

C. *Petrus Damiani* (*d.* 1072): *State and Church* (*Two Swords*) [2]

Either dignity is in need of the other: while the priesthood is protected by the watchfulness (*tuitio*) of the king, the kingdom is likewise supported by the holiness of the sacerdotal office. (Epist. III, 6.)

---

[1] Translated by H. W. from *Epistola ad Leonem III papam, ibid.*, no. 238, p. 118.

[2] Translated by H. W. from *Petrus Damiani: Staat und Kirche, ibid.*, no. 277, p. 145.

The offices of kingship and priesthood are clearly distinguished from each other in this way, that the king makes use of secular arms and that the priest is armed with the sword of the spirit which is the Word of the Lord. (Epist. IV, 9.)

Mankind will be blessed if the sword of the kingdom be united with the sword of priesthood so that the sword of the priest may soften the sword of the king and the sword of the king may sharpen the sword of the priest. Then the kingdom will prosper, priesthood will thrive and both will be honored since they will be united in a happy alliance willed by God. (Sermo 69.)

D. *Dante Alighieri (d. 1321) on Pope and Emperor*[1]

Rome which made the world good used to have two suns to point out both paths, that of the world and that of God. One has suppressed the other, and the sword is joined with the shepherd's crook[2] and of necessity they go badly together since, combined, one cannot check the other. (*Divine Comedy,* Purgatory XVI, 106-112).

— Reading No. 17 —

THE REVIVAL OF LEARNING

The revival of cultural life in the Frankish kingdom has two separate but interrelated aspects: one is Charles's great project to establish for his whole kingdom a system of monastic and cathedral schools to train the present and

[1] Dante, *The Divine Comedy.* A new prose translation . . . by H. R. Huse (New York, Rinehart, 1954), pp. 244-245.
[2] Here Dante refers to the spiritual "sword" as the pastoral staff.

future ministers of God, the teachers and scholars— places where high standards of scholarship would secure the correct transmission of the texts and rituals that underlie the ceremonies and instructions of the Christian faith. This great program of Charles and the scholars of his entourage is best represented in the capitularies, general exhortations, and letters issued to his officials on these matters (17A-D).

The second aspect is Charles's achievement in transforming the old palace school of the Merovingians into a kind of Academy with the purpose of providing instruction to the young noblemen and commoners living at the court, to train some of the more gifted ones for positions in schools all over the empire and to foster literary and scholarly activities among its members. In addition to formal instruction in some or all of the branches of Liberal Arts the palace school also conveyed a more informal instruction to more advanced students of all ages, including the king himself. At first, the school traveled with the king and his household; later it was permanently fixed to Charles's residence at Aachen. Its titular head was the Anglo-Saxon scholar Alcuin. From his bulky correspondence we give in this Reading some excerpts from his letters to King Charles. They call attention to the great variety of the intellectual activities of Charles and his scholars, which were marked, so it seems, at least as much by a great eagerness to absorb "the sciences" for their own sake, as by an interest in their practical adaptability (17E). Above all, Alcuin's letters show the genuine effort of this group to restore the purity and beauty of the Latin language and style in the image of the best writers of the past to whose study they devoted much of their time and energies.

As to the general character of the literature produced in vast amounts during this period most of the works are either commentaries on books of Holy Scriptures and on the Church Fathers, or they are concerned with the Liberal Arts. In short, they show a practical bent. Some of them are written in form of dialogues between master and pupils, thus betraying their intimate connection with class instruction (17F and 17G). The masters tried to

*convey to their pupils the concrete meaning of words by
way of definitions and associations rather than by developing thought and skill in argument. Intellectual creative-
ness was not a special characteristic of this period, which
is fittingly described by H. O. Taylor as the first phase of
the development of the "Mind of the Middle Ages,"—a period when scholars appropriated the means and tools of
learning from a greater and richer past in preparation for
higher pursuits to come. In line with this the greatest emphasis is on grammar. "Grammar," says Alcuin, "is the
science of letters and the guardian of right speech and
writing; it depends on nature, reason, authority, and custom."*

*In the field of poetry, however, some Carolingian writ-
ers were able to set much higher standards. It is remarkable how, for instance, a Theodulf of Orleans, in spite of
the strait jacket imposed by his devotion to the ancient
metres, could let his pen expand freely on his own experi-
ences and on scenes from life. See the charming description (17н) of court life at Charles's palace in Aachen
(inserted in a long poem) with which we conclude this
Reading.*

✓　　　　✓　　　　✓

A. *Capitulary on Education* (De litteris colendis)[1]

Be it known, therefore, to your devotion pleasing to
God, that we, together with our faithful, have considered
it to be useful that the bishoprics and monasteries entrusted by the favor of Christ to our control, in addition
to the order of monastic life and the intercourse of holy
religion, also ought to be zealous in the culture of letters,
teaching those who by the gift of God are able to learn,
according to the capacity of each individual. Just
as the observance of the rule imparts order and grace to
honesty and morals, so also zeal in teaching and learning
may do the same for sentences, so that those who desire
to please God by living rightly should not neglect to
please him also by speaking correctly. For it is written:

[1] From University of Pennsylvania, *Translations and Reprints,*
VI, 5, pp. 12-14.

"Either from thy words thou shalt be justified or from thy words thou shalt be condemned." [1] . . . For when in the years just passed letters were often written to us from several monasteries in which it was stated that the brethren who dwelt there offered up in our behalf sacred and pious prayers, we have recognized in most of these letters both correct thought and uncouth expressions: because what pious devotion dictated faithfully to the mind, the tongue, uneducated on account of the neglect of study, was not able to express in a letter without error. Whence it happened that we began to fear lest perchance, as the skill in writing was less, so also the wisdom for understanding the Holy Scriptures might be much less than it rightly ought to be. And we all know well that, although errors of speech are dangerous, far more dangerous are errors of the understanding. Therefore, we exhort you not only not to neglect the study of letters, but also with most humble mind, pleasant to God, to study earnestly in order that you may be able more easily and more correctly to penetrate the mysteries of the divine Scriptures. Since, moreover, images, tropes, and similar figures are found in the sacred pages, no one doubts that each one on reading these will understand the spiritual sense more quickly if previously he shall have been fully instructed in the mastery of letters. Such men truly are to be chosen for this work as have both the will and the ability to learn and a desire to instruct others. And may this be done with a zeal as great as the earnestness with which we command it. For we desire you to be, as it is fitting that soldiers of the church should, devout in mind, learned in discourse, chaste in conduct and eloquent in speech, so that whosoever shall seek to see you out of reverence for God, or on account of your reputation for holy conduct, just as he is edified by your appearance, may also be instructed by your wisdom, which he has learned from your reading or singing, and may go away joyfully giving thanks to omnipotent God. Do not neglect, therefore, if you wish to have our favor, to send copies of this letter to all your suffragans and fellow-bishops and to all the monasteries.

[1] Matthew, xii, 37.

B. *From* Admonitio Generalis, 789 [1]

CH. 72. And we also demand of your holiness that the ministers of the altar of God shall adorn their ministry by good manners, and likewise the other orders who observe a rule and the congregations of monks. We implore them to lead a just and fitting life, just as God Himself commanded in the Gospel [Matthew, v.16]: "Let your light so shine before men that they may see your good works and glorify your Father which is in heaven," so that by their example many may be led to serve God; and let them join and associate to themselves not only children of servile condition, but also sons of free men. And let schools be established in which boys may learn to read. Correct carefully the Psalms, the signs in writing (*notas*), the songs, the calendar, the grammar, in each monastery or bishopric, and the Catholic books: because often some desire to pray to God properly, but they pray badly because of the incorrect books. And do not permit your boys to corrupt them in reading or writing. If there is need of writing the Gospel, Psalter and Missal, let men of mature age do the writing with all diligence.

C. *From* Capitularies to the Missi[2]

803.2. Priests shall not be ordained without an examination. And excommunication shall not be ordered at random and without cause.

802-813.2. We will and command that laymen shall learn thoroughly the creed and the Lord's prayer.

D. *The Revival of Church Music and Ritual*

From the Annals of Lorsch, 757 [3]

Emperor Constantine sent Pepin along with other gifts an organ which arrived in Frankland in due time.

From a General Letter of King Charles, 768-800 [4]

[1] *Ibid.,* p. 15.
[2] *Ibid.,* p. 15-16.
[3] From the *Annales Laureshamenses* (*Mon. Germ. Hist., Scriptores* I), p. 140.
[4] From University of Pennsylvania, *Translations and Reprints,* VI, 5, pp. 14-15.

Charles, confiding in the aid of God, King of the Franks and Lombards, and Patrician of the Romans, to the religious lectors subject to our power. . . . Incited . . . by the example of our father Pipin, of venerated memory, who by his zeal decorated all the churches of the Gauls with the songs of the Roman Church, we are careful by our skill to make these churches illustrious by a series of excellent lectionaries. Finally, because we have found the lectionaries for the nocturnal offices, compiled by the fruitless labor of certain ones, in spite of their correct intention, unsuitable because they were written without the words of their authors and were full of an infinite number of errors, we cannot suffer in our days discordant solecisms to glide into the sacred lessons among the holy offices, and we purpose to improve these lessons. And we have entrusted this work to Paul the deacon, our friend and client. We have directed him to peruse carefully the sayings of the Catholic Fathers and to choose, so to speak, from the most broad meadows of their writing certain flowers, and from the most useful to form, as it were, a single garland. He, desiring to obey devoutly our highness, has read through the treatises and sermons of the different Catholic fathers, has chosen from each the best and has presented to us in two volumes lessons suitable for the whole year and for each separate festival, and free from error. We have examined the text of all these with our wisdom, we have established these volumes by our authority, and we deliver them to your religion to be read in the churches of Christ.

E. *From Letters by Alcuin to King Charles,*[1]
799.

Most venerable and devout king, we thank you for allowing our book, which you commanded us to write and send, to be read out to you; we also thank you for drawing attention to our mistakes and returning the book for correction, although you would have been much better qualified to correct these mistakes; it very often happens that the judgment of an outsider is more valuable than that of the author himself. . . .

[1] Translated by H. F. Orton, from *Alcuini Epistolae* (*Mon. Germ. Hist., Epistolae* IV), nos. 172, 148, pp. 284-285, 239.

I have not seen the "Disputation between Felix and the Saracen," nor can I find it in our library; indeed, I had not even heard of his name. Then I made further careful inquiry whether any member of our household had any information about this book and I was told I might find it in the possession of Leidrad, the bishop of Lyons. I speedily sent my messenger to the bishop and told him to despatch the book, if it were found, as quickly as possible.

When as a young man I went to Rome and was staying for a few days in the royal city of Pavia there was a Jew called Lullus who disputed with Master Peter (of Pisa): I have heard that there exists in that city a written account of this disputation. He is the same Peter who has now become famous as a teacher of grammar at your palace. Perhaps your "Homer" (Angilbert) has heard the above-named master speak about this.

I have sent your Excellency some specimens of style, which are backed by the authority of examples or verses of the venerable father [Master Peter]; for your enjoyment I have added some subtle formulae of arithmetic on the tablet which was blank when you sent it; it was bare when I first saw it and now I have clothed it and return it to you. Indeed, I think it is fit that this tablet which came to us ennobled by your seal should thus be further honored by our literary composition. And in case I have left out any type of style among the examples which I have selected, Beselel [Einhard], our mutual friend and partner in work could add some verse written by the same father. Moreover, he can also give his opinion on the calculations contained in my book on arithmetic.

Clauses and sub-clauses correctly punctuated give an extremely fine polish to a sentence; but authors are no longer familiar with them on account of their lack of erudition. But your noble efforts have now brought about a re-birth of civilised standards in every kind of knowledge and of useful erudition. Therefore it seems to me highly desirable that writers should again learn to phrase their sentences correctly.

As far as I am concerned I am engaged in a daily struggle against the illiteracy which prevails at Tours— although progress is rather slow. I can only wish that your authority may stimulate the education of the children at the palace; they should reproduce in their best style the lucid words by which you convey your thought so that, wherever the king's writ runs, it should display the nobleness of the king's wisdom.

798.

My teacher used to tell me: "The wisest of all men were those who discovered this art (astronomy) in the concrete facts of nature. It would be a great shame if we let it perish in our own days."—But the narrowmindedness of many scholars does not care for the comprehension of things of nature, which God has created. You know full well how sweet arithmetic is in its calculations, how necessary for the understanding of sacred scriptures, how pleasant the knowledge of the heavenly bodies and their revolutions. But those who care to know such matters are rare; and, what is worse, students refuse to study them.

F. *Alcuin:* On Grammar[1]

In Albinus' [Alcuin's] school, there were two boys, one a Frank, the other a Saxon; they had recently mastered the first rudiments of grammar. Therefore they decided to rehearse their few scraps of literary knowledge by asking each other questions to test their memory.

First the Frank said to the Saxon:

"Well, my Saxon friend; you answer my questions because you are older. I am fourteen; you are fifteen, I think."

The Saxon replied:

"Yes, I will do this: but on condition that we may consult the Master if any question should arise which is beyond our understanding, or which requires a knowledge of philosophy."

"All right boys," said the Master, "this is a sound suggestion, and I willingly agree. But first of all, tell me: which do you think is the best point for starting your debate?"

[1] Translated by H. F. Orton from *Alcuini Opera,* Migne, *Patr. Lat.* CI, cols. 854, 862-863.

PUPIL: The letters [of the alphabet] of course, Sir.

MASTER: This answer would be right if you had not just brought up the subject of philosophy. As it is, you must start your debate with a definition of words for the sake of which letters have been invented. Better still, we should first ask ourselves: What are the different aspects of a debate?

PUPIL: Sir, we humbly beg you to explain this to us; we must admit that we do not know the aspects of a debate.

MASTER: Every sentence and argument consists of three parts: things, intellect and words. A thing is what we are first aware of; then we learn to understand its nature by the operation of our intellect; finally we express it by words: and for the sake of words letters have been invented." . . .

FRANK: How can I know which gender any word is?

SAXON: There are definite rules about various endings of words which indicate the gender a word might be— but to go through these rules would take a long time and be rather tedious in a debate between boys such as this.

FRANK: But I have already told you.

SAXON: So what?

FRANK: So what? You are only envious because I know more.

SAXON: Certainly not, brother: but I wanted to check your greed for showing off.

FRANK: So you want to check my greed—but what about your own stubbornness?

SAXON: Well, carry on: I shall stick to your plan.

G. *From a Brief Dialogue Entitled* The Dispute of the Most Noble Young Prince Pepin with his Master Alcuin[1]

P. What is a letter?	A. The guardian of history.
P. What is a word?	A. The mind's betrayer.
P. What created a word?	A. The tongue.
P. What is the tongue?	A. Something that whips the air.
P. What is the air?	A. The protection of life.

[1] Quoted in L. Laistner, *Thought and Letters in Western Europe, A.D. 400-900,* new ed. (London 1951), p. 199.

P. What is life?   A. The joy of the blessed, the sorrow of sinners, the expectation of death.

P. What is death?   A. An unavoidable occurrence, an uncertain journey, the tears of the living, the confirmation of the testament, the thief of man.

P. What is man?   A. The slave of death, a passing wayfarer, the guest of a place.

P. To what is man like?   A. A fruit [homo—pomo; the Latin play of words cannot be rendered].

P. Where is he situated?   A. Within six walls.

P. Which?   A. Above, below, before, behind, right and left.

P. In how many ways does he vary?   A. In hunger and satiety, repose and labour, in wakeful hours and sleep.

P. What is sleep?   A. The image of death.

H. *From the Poem,* Ad Carolum Regem, *by Theodulf of Orleans*[1]

Behold, the year renews its joyful season according to nature's eternal laws and mother Earth brings forth her flowers . . . now is the time to hold the solemn assembly; now is the time for prayers in the royal palace, where a fine building rises with its wonderful dome. From there, back to the height of the king's residence; let the people pace up and down the long corridors outside; now let the gate be opened: many wish to enter, but only a few are admitted—the few privileged by their rank.

The beloved children surround the splendid king; as the sun in the sky, so the king outshines them all. Next to him stand the boys, while the girls form a circle round him; they gladden the father's heart like fresh shoots of

[1] Translated by H. F. Orton from *Poetae Latini aevi Karolini* (*Mon. Germ. Hist., Poetae Latini* I), pp. 485-487, vv. 53-54, 61-80, 91-96, 131-134, 155-157.

vine. Let Charles stand here next to Lewis: one already a
young man, the other's face showing the first down of
manhood. Both are very strong in body with youthful
sinews, endowed with a good mind and sturdy in counsel.
Their intellect is vigorous, their prowess renowned, their
charity abundant; each the pride of his kinsmen, each the
joy of his father. Now the king casts his loving glances on
these boys, now he turns to the maidens surrounding him
on each side—that group of maidens unsurpassed as regards attire, appearance, beauty, form, heart and religion.
The charming children are ready to render pleasant services to their father; in loving devotion they vie with one
another who shall please him best. Charles might quickly
release him of his wide cloak and smooth gloves while
Lewis takes his sword. . . . Once the king is seated, his
virtuous daughters may offer their pleasant gifts [of flowers and fruit] and thereby show their loving care.

Flaccus (Alcuin) should be present, the glory of our
bards, who is capable of singing on many a theme in
lyrical metres with a powerful voice. He also is an acute
philosopher, a melodic poet, vigorous in thought and
strong in deed.

Nardulus (Einhard) strides back and forth without
respite; your foot comes and goes as if you were an ant
—a small body which houses a great spirit.

— Reading No. 18 —

GROWTH OF VERNACULAR
CULTURES

*While Charlemagne's attempt to save for posterity some
of the heroic lays of the ancient Germans (18A) was
doomed to failure his endeavors to bring the teachings
and documents of Christianity closer to the people by the
use of their own native languages met with lasting success. The king ordered that every layman "shall learn the
creed and the Lord's prayer" that is to say in his own
language.* (See Reading No. 18C.) *As an example of
the way this knowledge was imposed on the catechumen
we bring here one of the simple questionnaires (18B) used
by the priest to make sure that the confessing candidate
knew not only what he had to believe but also what he
had to abjure.*

*Later, and as an integrated part of his entire cultural
and educational program, Charles encouraged German
translations of the gospels and of homilies, along with
commentaries and glosses on the sacred texts. This was
to help implement his order to the clergy throughout his
empire (18C) that they should preach to the peoples in
their own respective vernacular.*

*How intimately these activities were related to the gen-
eral revival of learning can be gleaned from the fact that
they arose and flourished at the very same monastic
schools that had developed into leading centers of liberal
arts and theological studies, such as St. Gall, Reichenau,
Murbach, and, especially, Fulda. It is therefore not surprising that the two German poets who undertook for the
first time to compose religious epics based on the Gospels
in the vernacular, the author of the Old Low German*

(*Saxon*) Heliand *and Otfrid of Weissenburg, who composed the* Gospel Book *in Old High German (Frankish), were both deeply influenced by these studies. Otfrid, so he tells us, chose the vernacular for his religious poem to replace what he called "the offensive songs of the layman," that is, pagan and secular lays, with religious verse in the layman's own language. In the first chapter of his* Gospel Book *he announces his intention to raise the German language to the literary dignity and standards of the "noble tongues" (edilzungun) in which God had hitherto revealed his truth and his will to mankind (18D).*

In spite of Charlemagne's attempts to unify the various peoples under his sway the forces that made for diversity were strongly at work. To the east and west of the boundary that was later to become the political boundary between eastern and western Franconia (Germany and France), the German and the Romance vernaculars came to their own and helped to express these divisions. The famous Strasburg Oaths (18E) of 842 demonstrate that by thirty years after Charlemagne's death the linguistic divisions of the empire had already become fixed on a geographical basis.

✓   ✓   ✓

A. *The Historian Einhard on Charlemagne's Interest in German Folk Tradition and Language*[1]

29. . . . He [Charles] . . . caused the unwritten laws of all the nations under his rule to be tabulated and reduced to writing. He also wrote out and committed to memory the rude and very ancient songs which told of the exploits and wars of the kings of old. He also began a grammar of the speech of his country. Likewise he gave names in the national tongue to the months of the year, for up to this time the Franks had distinguished them partly by Latin and partly by barbarian names. He likewise gave the proper names to the twelve winds, for previously names were known for hardly four. . . .

[1] From *Life of the Emperor Karl the Great,* translated from Eginhard by William Glaister (London, 1877), pp. 84, 85.

B. *A Formula of Baptismal Confession Imposed upon the Saxons*[1]

INTERROGATIO SACERDOTIS [the questioning of the priest]

[Original Old German version:]

Forsahhistu unholdun? Ih fursahu.

Forsahhistu unholdun werk indi willon? Ih fursahhu.

Forsahhistu allem them bluostrum indi den gelton, indi den gotum thie im heidene man zi bluostrum indi zi geldom enti zi gotum habent? Ih fursahhu.

Gilaubistu in Got fater almahtigan? Ih gilaubu.

Gilaubistu in Christ Gotes sun nerienton? Ih gilaubu.

Gilaubistu in heiligan geist? Ih gilaubu.

Gilaubistu einan Got almahtigan in thrinisse inti in einisse? Ih gilaubu.

Gilaubistu heilage Gotes chirichun? Ih gilaubu.

Gilaubistu thuruh taufunga sunteano forlaznessi? Ih gilaubu.

Gilaubistu lib after tode? Ih gilaubu.[2]

[English version:]

Do you forswear the demons? I do. Do you forswear all works and purposes of the demons? I do. Do you forswear all sacrifices, idols and gods whom the heathen have as their sacrifices, idols and gods? I do, Do you believe in God, the Almighty? I do. Do you believe in Christ, son of God, the redeemer? I do. Do you believe in the Holy Ghost? I do. Do you believe in an almighty God, in trinity and in unity? I do. Do you believe in the

---

[1] From E. v. Steinmeyer, *Die kleineren althochdeutschen Sprachdenkmäler* (Berlin, 1916), p. 23.

[2] A modern German version would read: Entsagest Du dem Bösen? Ich entsage. Entsagst Du dem Werk und Willen des Bösen? Ich entsage. Entsagest Du allen Opfern, Götzenbildern und Götzen, die die Heiden als Opfer, Götzenbilder und Götzen, für sich haben? Ich entsage. Glaubst Du an Gottvater, den Allmächtigen? Ich glaube. Glaubst Du an Christus, Gottes Sohn, den Heiland? Ich glaube. Glaubst Du an den heiligen Geist? Ich glaube. Glaubst Du an einen allmächtigen Gott in Dreiheit und in Einheit? Ich glaube. Glaubst Du an Gottes heilige Kirche? Ich glaube. Glaubst Du an die Vergebung der Sünden durch die Taufe? Ich glaube. Glaubst Du an ein Leben nach dem Tod? Ich glaube.

Holy Church of God? I do. Do you believe in the remission of sins through baptism? I do. Do you believe in life after death? I do.

c. *From the Decrees of the Council of Tours, 813* [1]

17. . . . Each priest should have a collection of homilies [sermons] containing all the necessary admonitions for the instruction of our subjects in the Catholic faith. . . . And each should see to it to have these homilies openly translated into the rustic Romance or German language (*Romanam aut Thiotiscam linguam*) so that all the people may well understand their content.

D *Why the Author* (*Otfrid of Weissenburg*) *Wrote his Book in German* (theotisce, "deutsch") [2]

Why should the Franks alone not try to sing God's praise in the Frankish language? Although not used for this kind of hymns and never developed according to rules, the language does not lack directness and beautiful simplicity. Just apply yourself with industry to make her sound in a lovely way and to make her express in splendid tones the greatness of God's commands. Thus songs in this metre will be praised for their beauty. We are sure of salvation if we understand God's word rightly. May it always please you to sing according to the rules set for the feet and metres; they are the rules of God himself. And if you desire to apply the metrical rules and to excel in your own tongue then try to fulfil at all times God's will. Thus the teaching of God's servants (the apostles) will also be read in Frankish verse. . . . Why should the Frank be rude and clumsy only in this one thing? Since he is keen and gallant like the Romans, he should be able to sing lofty songs in his own language. Neither should one say that the Greeks outdo the Franks in prowess. They are endowed with the same wisdom and use it to their profit.

[1] Translated by H. W. from *Concilia aevi Karolini* I (*Mon. Germ. Hist., Legum Sectio* III, 2), p. 288.

[2] Adapted with the help of a modern German version from *Otfrid's Evangelienbuch*, herausgegeben von P. Piper, vol. I (Freiburg, 1882), I, 1, vv., 33-45, 57-61 (pp. 21, 22-23).

E. *The Strasburg Oaths,* 842 [1]

ROMANCE VERSION

Pro Deo amur et pro Christian poblo et nostro commun salvament dist di in avant, in quant Deus savir et podir me dunat, si salvarai eo cist meon fradre Karlo et in adiudha et in cadhuna cosa, si cum om per dreit son fradre salvar dist, in o quid il mi altresi fazet; et ab Ludher nul plaid numquam prindrai, qui meon vol cist meon fradre Karlo in damno sit.

GERMAN VERSION

In Godes minna ind in thes Christianes folches ind unser bedhero gealtnissi, fon thesemo dage frammordes, so fram so mir Got gewizci indi madh furgibit, so haldih thesan minan bruodher soso man mit rehtu sinan bruodher scal, in thiu, thaz er mig so sama duo; indi mit Ludheren in nohheiniu thing ne gegango, the minan willon imo ce scadhen werben.

IN ENGLISH [2]

For the love of God and the common salvation of the Christian people and from this day on, as far as God gives me wisdom and power, I will treat this my brother as one should rightfully treat a brother, on condition that he does the same by me. And with Lothair I will not willingly enter into any agreement which might injure this my brother.

[1] The Oaths are found in the Chronicle of Nithard: *Nithardi Historiarum libri* IV. Edition by G. H. Pertz (Hannover, 1870), III, 5, pp. 38-39.
[2] From J. R. Strayer, *The Middle Ages,* 4th ed. (New York, 1959), p. 103.

THE REVIVAL OF ART

To give an idea of the intentions and tastes of the ruler, the account of Einhard (19A) is quite helpful. Einhard makes the point that native materials were supplemented by imports from Rome and Ravenna. This holds true also of artistic ideas and forms. Roman influence was not restricted to contemporary Rome, with its Byzantine and Christian art, but included also the ruins, monuments, and churches in the old Roman provinces of Charlemagne's empire. Ravenna, on the other hand, symbolizes Byzantine as well as Germanic tradition. Charles had the statue of the Ostrogoth Theodoric carried to Frankland and set up before his palace in Aachen. For the decorative arts craftsmen mostly borrowed from eastern models, but transformed them in their own Teutonic way. In his report Einhard does not mention book illumination though this is one of the glories of the Carolingian period. Works like Charlemagne's "Golden Gospels" mingled influences from England with those from the South and the East.

Another help for the understanding of the inclusion of art into Charles's program of intellectual, educational, and religious revival is provided by the Libri Carolini, the authoritative work on images and image worship composed by Charles's scholars. If pieced together, the pertinent passages in the book form what we would call a discussion of the aesthetical and practical values of art. No doubt, the formulation was influenced by ancient theories, but it reflects also in a most lively way the urgent need for clarification and definition of the nature of images stirred up by the theological struggle about image worship. In accordance with their conviction that the adoration of images was "wicked" and images should be destroyed, the Carolingian scholars had to prove that nothing supernatural or sacramental went into the making of pictures. Images were simply man-made. The same stand-

ards of technical skill and of beautiful and eye-pleasing forms had to be applied to them as were required of the products of all arts and crafts. The painter deals with colors and design and creates without the assistance of the Holy Spirit. Art has to serve man in his physical life in the same way as the sacraments serve him in his metaphysical endeavors. In this respect images perform the double function of embellishing man's surroundings, especially his places of worship, and of keeping alive the memory of the saints as examples of a God-pleasing life. To do so they had to be articulate and realistic. Thus the theory fits the practice of Carolingian art, which reintroduced "the human body in its full three-dimensional reality," replacing in part the abstract and ornamental style of the migration period. Some excerpts from the Libri Carolini are included here (19B).

✓   ✓   ✓

A. *Einhard on Charlemagne's Building and Artistic Activities*[1]

17. Illustrious as the king was in the work of enlarging his kingdom and in conquering foreign nations, and though so constantly occupied with such affairs, he nevertheless began in several places very many works for the advantage and beautifying of his kingdom. Some of these he was able to finish. Chief among them may be mentioned, as deserving of notice, the Basilica of the Holy Mother of God, built at Aachen, a marvel of workmanship; and the bridge over the Rhine at Mainz, five hundred paces in length; so broad is the river at that place. This bridge, however, was destroyed by fire the year before the king died, nor could it be restored on account of his approaching death, although it was in the king's mind to replace the wooden structure by a bridge of stone.

He also began some magnificent palaces, one not far from Mainz, near the village of Ingelheim, and another at Nymwegen, on the river Waal, which flows past the island of the Batavians on the southern side. He was more especially particular in giving orders to priests and fathers

[1] From *Life of the Emperor Karl the Great,* translated from Eginhard by William Glaister (London, 1877), pp. 63, 64, 78, 79, 80.

to see to the restoration of those churches under their
care, which in any part of his kingdom he found had
fallen into decay, taking care by his officers that his commands were obeyed. . . .

26. The Christian religion in which he had been brought
up from infancy was held by Charles as most sacred, and
he worshipped in it with the greatest piety. For this reason
he built at Aachen a most beautiful church, which he enriched with gold and silver and candlesticks, and also with
lattices and doors of solid brass. When columns and mar-
bles for the building could not be obtained from elsewhere,
he had them brought from Rome and Ravenna. . . .

He provided for the church an abundance of sacred
vessels of gold and silver, and priestly vestments, so that
when service was celebrated it was not necessary even for
the doorkeepers, who are the lower order of ecclesiastics,
to perform their duties in private dress. . . .

27. . . . He held the church of the blessed Peter the
apostle, at Rome, in far higher regard than any other
place of sanctity and veneration, and he enriched its
treasury with a great quantity of gold, silver, and precious
stones. . . .

B. *On the Art of Painting and on Pictures. From the*
Libri Carolini[1]

. . . Pictures are neither in need of the mysterious
imposing of hands nor of consecration; all they need is
to be formed and put together by those who have the full
experience of the art of painting and of the mixing of
colors; or else by those who are experts in work of metal,
stone or wood or any other such art and who carve out
faces in these materials. Nor indeed is there any priest
present at their so-called consecration who evokes the
memory of Christ's passion . . . and who prays intently
to have them carried by angels to the celestial altar and
before the presence of the divine majesty. But here we
have only the painter looking for a place well suited to
perform the work and only anxious to achieve beauty
and to improve its look. . . .

[1] Translated by H.W. from the *Libri Carolini* ed. H. Bastgen
    (*Mon. Germ. Hist., Legum sectio* III, *Concilia* II, *Sup-
    plementum*), II, 27, pp. 88, 89.

The sacrament differs from pictures painted by the artist in more respects than can be explained reasonably: the former is performed invisibly by the working of the spirit of God, the latter visibly by the hand of the artist; the former is consecrated by the priest, the latter are painted by the painter who possesses only human skill and knowledge; the former is carried by angelic hands to the sublime altar of God, the latter are created artificially by human hands and painted on walls to be seen by beholders; the former is instrumental in remitting sins, the latter if used indiscriminately add to sins; the former does neither increase nor decrease in virtue; the latter's beauty can increase and in some way decrease depending upon the taste and ingenuity of the artist; . . . the former is nourishment for the soul, the latter is food only for the eyes; by its intake the former leads to the entrance of the celestial kingdom; the latter transmits the memory of the deeds [of the saints] to the beholder. . . .

BIBLIOGRAPHY

Buckler, F. W. *Harunu'l-Rashid and Charles the Great,* 1931.

Byzantium: An Introduction to East Roman Civilization. Ed. by N. H. Baynes and H. S. L. Moss. Oxford, 1948.

The Cambridge Economic History of Europe. Vol. I. Cambridge, 1941.

"The Coronation of Charlemagne—What Did It Signify?" In: *Problems of European Civilization.* Boston (D. C. Heath & Co.), 1959.

Dalton, O. M. *The History of the Franks by Gregory of Tours,* Vol. 1, Introduction. Oxford, 1927.

Davis, H. W. C. *Charlemagne, the Hero of two Nations.* London, New York, 1900.

Dill, S. *Roman Society in Gaul in the Merovingian Age.* London, 1926.

Dopsch, A. *The Economic and Social Foundations of European Civilization.* New York, 1937.

Duckett, E. S. *Alcuin, Friend of Charlemagne.* New York, 1951.

Fichtenau, H. *The Carolingian Empire.* Translated by P. Muntz. Oxford, 1957.

Ganshof, F. L. "Charlemagne," *Speculum,* Vol. XXIV (1949), pp. 520-528.

Halphen, L. *Charlemagne et l'Empire Carolingien.* Paris, 1947.

Hitti, P. K. *The Arabs: A Short History.* Princeton, 1943.

Hodgkin, Th. *Charles the Great,* London, 1897.

Kleinclausz, A. J. *Charlemagne.* Paris, 1934.

Laistner, M. L. W. *Thought and Letters in Western Europe.* New edition. Ithaca, N.Y., 1957.

"Laws of Charles the Great." In *Translations and Reprints from the Original Sources of European History.* Vol. VI, no. 5. University of Pennsylvania, Philadelphia, 1899.

The Letters of St. Boniface. Translated with an Introduction by Ephraim Emerton. New York, 1940.

Levison, William. *England and the Continent in the Eighth Century.* Oxford, 1946.

Early Lives of Charlemagne by Eginhard and the Monk of St. Gall. Translated by A. J. Grant. London, 1926.

Lot, F. *The End of the Ancient World and the Beginnings of the Middle Ages.* New York, 1931.

Moss, H. S. L. B. *The Birth of the Middle Ages.* London, 1935.

Pirenne, H. *Mohammed and Charlemagne.* London, 1939.

"The Pirenne Thesis—Analysis, Criticism and Revision." In: *Problems in European Civilization.* Boston (D. C. Heath & Co.), 1958.

Prévité Orton, C. W. *The Shorter Cambridge Medieval History,* Vol. I: *The Later Roman Empire to the Twelfth Century.* Cambridge, 1952.

The Rhetoric of Alcuin and Charlemagne. A translation with an Introduction, the Latin Text and Notes by W. S. Howell. Princeton, 1941.

Runciman, S. *Byzantine Civilization.* New York (Meridian Books), 1956.

Strayer, J. S. *The Middle Ages.* 4th ed. New York, 1959.

Wallach, L. *Alcuin and Charlemagne: Studies in Carolingian History and Literature.* Ithaca, N.Y., 1959.

West, A. F. *Alcuin and the Rise of Christian Schools.* New York, 1892.

Winston, R. *Charlemagne: From the Hammer to the Cross.* New York (Vintage Books), 1960.

INDEX